THE WINTER PEOPLE

THE
WINTER PEOPLE
A Return to Cape Cod

CHARLES N. BARNARD

DODD, MEAD & COMPANY
NEW YORK

ISBN: 0–396–06780–8
Library of Congress Catalog Card Number: 72–12435
Printed in the United States of America
by The Haddon Craftsmen, Inc., Scranton, Penna.

CONTENTS

6 CONTENTS

INTRODUCTION

THIS is not so much a book about Cape Cod as it is a personal story—I think it might be called a love story—which happens to take place on that defiant little piece of ocean-dominated real estate that makes a fist, bends its elbow, and flexes its bicep at the Atlantic Ocean off Massachusetts.

We all, I suppose, have a summer place in our lives, in our stories—a place of escape, of young, happy memories, of long days without harsh words, a place we once went deliberately to enjoy, a place with which we had a sort of secret and joyful covenant. Yours may be in the shadow of mountains, or on a farm, or by a lake. Mine was on Cape Cod.

Most of the books I have read about Cape Cod were written by experts, which I am not. The authors of these books were not just summer vacationers, as I was, but historians, naturalists, teachers, geologists, novelists, ornitholo-

gists, or philosophers. They were people who had lived a
calendar year in an "outermost house" on a Cape Cod
beach, as Henry Beston did, or walked the length of the
lower Cape as Thoreau did, or were descendants of first
families, like the Richardsons of Nauset Marsh. Some knew
the place from childhood and could claim knowledge of it
almost as a birthright. Some were indeed born there.

All of these writers are people of impressive and indisputa-
ble credentials. They have studied the Cape, interpreted the
Cape, described the Cape. They have often demonstrated
deep instincts about the mystique of this place. For the most
part, and rightly so, such writers are accepted as a part of
the Cape's elite; even when their names are not Nickerson
or Snow, they are respected as if they were Cape-born, for
they have certified their love of what some people call the
Narrow Land; they have contributed to its fame, its legends,
its charm, and thereby, whether they intended or not, to its
economic well-being.

I think there will always be enough people qualified by
birth, intellect, prose style, and motive to write all the books
that will ever need to be written about Cape Cod. Indeed,
many residents of this sandy peninsula wish that no more be
written about the place at all, that no more descriptions of
its charms be broadcast, no more paintings of its cottages
and its fishing boats painted, no more photographs of its
sands and its sunsets printed, no more "Bury My Heart On
Old Cape Cod" songs composed, no more brochures distributed by travel agents, no more efforts made by Massa-

chusetts to attract retirement families; in short, that the money and the bulldozers and campers and motel operators and road builders and artists and gift shops and hippies— yes, particularly the damned hippies—would go away and leave the Cape to its own people to enjoy.

Well, in writing this book, it isn't my purpose to further promote Cape Cod in any commercial, touristic sense, and it certainly isn't my expectation to rival the Bestons and the Thoreaus and the Kittredges who have chronicled the Cape's history and its geology, its flora and fauna, and its famed state of mind.

This book will be something different. It may be the first book to be written about the Cape by one of those usually despised but annually tolerated "summer people."

It is said that the caste system on the Cape is like a pyramid with the summer people at the base. At the top, at the point, are the first families—Nickersons, Snows, Bradfords, Doanes, and all the others who have been there since the beginning—good people, spare, taciturn, honest, hard working, likeable, thrifty, able: a sort of indigenous aristocracy of the land, some of them Mayflower descendants, some almost.

Next come the old Yankee families from Massachusetts who have been migrating to the Cape every summer since Coolidge's time and before, who built solid summer places in the towns along the bay and who became almost as much an organic part of the Cape's social structure as the seventeenth-century originals.

After these patriarchal families, in order of dignity and prestige, there are the other Cape Codders who have been around the peninsula so long, like the Portuguese fishermen of Provincetown and the Indian families of Mashpee, and have made enough of a contribution to the arts and to commerce to be accepted as members of the year-round lodge.

Finally, there are the summer people, those great motorized battalions who come between July Fourth and Labor Day and who are the economic lifeblood of the Cape, the people who rent the cottages, patronize the restaurants and supermarkets and liquor stores, who buy the beach stickers, clog the highways, take every uncomfortable seat in the summer theaters, line up at the gas pumps for fuel and at the air pumps to inflate their beach toys, who litter the beaches, exasperate the police, fill the air with kites, Frisbees and exhaust fumes, glut the parking lots, buy the oil paintings and salt-water taffy, lose their children and pets, photograph the windmills and the fishing boats, sleep on the beaches, visit the kiddielands and the aquariums, stock up on bayberry candles and beach-plum jelly, complain about the summer fogs, take sightseeing airplane rides, scratch about in the mud flats for clams, rent bicycles, hire babysitters, take sunset tours through the sands in dune buggies, buy up all the *Wall Street Journals* and *New York Timeses*, exhaust the supplies of suntan lotion, kite string, and insect spray, and finally, go home each year, sunburned, exhausted and broke, leaving millions of dollars in the hands of the natives.

Summer people come from everywhere; some days you can count license plates from twenty states before noon. A few come only once, but many more come again. They are, for the most part, at least modestly affluent, or they wouldn't visit Cape Cod in the first place; it isn't cheap. They are upper-middle-class Americans with tastes to match; it isn't Coney Island. When you meet them on the beaches, they are friendly, enthusiastic, full of the secure happiness of parents who watch their little, sunbrowned kids running around in the salt air. Cape Cod, they always say, is *such* a wonderful place. Sometimes they add, "I wonder what it's like around here in the winter," but only as a passing thought. I used to say it too, sometimes.

For about fourteen summers, I was one of these people, a member of the Cape's great transient majority, one of the tens of thousands of July-and-August faces-without-names. And if I didn't have a name as far as the Cape was concerned, neither did the Cape people I saw each year have names either. The man in the small supermarket in Eastham. The art gallery owner. The National Park ranger. After fourteen years, of course, I told myself that I knew the Cape. Actually, what I knew was its places, not its people. I knew July but not October, I knew August but not February.

Then one year, everything changed. There would be no planning and packing that summer, no lists of what to bring, no horseshoes, dartboard, scuba masks, red plastic air mattresses; no duffel bag full of linens, potty seat, swing, TV antenna, crib, kites, bedtime story books. No roof rack overloaded, no long ride from Connecticut, no joy of anticipation, no joy of arrival. Our Cape Cod idyll was ended.

When I lost the Cape I had known and loved, I felt I must have some token to take its place. I set out to find a new Cape Cod, the one I had missed, the one that is always there even when the summer people are not, a Cape Cod we had never known.

"I wonder what it's like in the winter, Dad?" the kids used to ask.

Now I would find out.

THE CANAL

ONE of the rituals of our annual migration to Eastham was to stop the car briefly at one of the parking areas along Route 6 beside the Cape Cod Canal. Not just any of the parking places, either, but one that came to be known as Number Four, the one which long years of experience had shown to have the best view of the canal, the best green area for kids to stretch cramped legs. A sign there explains that the canal is seventeen miles long, "the longest sea-level canal in the world," that it is maintained by the U.S. Army Corps of Engineers, that it is so many feet deep and wide and so forth. Each year some of us would stand there stretching the kinks out of our backs and read that same dopey sign as if we had never seen those dull facts before. It wasn't that we ever cared about the information, rather it was a tradition, like putting a certain ornament on the Christmas tree each year.

Another part of the tradition of Number Four was to break out some cold drinks and paper cups and refresh our road-weary throats—a couple of good Tuborg beers for the adults, Coke for the kids. We would also try to make our cat take a drink of ice water, but good old solid-black Nidge, curled up on a duffel bag in the back of the car, always refused. No matter, we knew we were now only forty-five minutes from our destination. I would check my watch and the mileage and say something about how well we had done this year and then we would all pile back into the car and head for the bridge.

There are two highway bridges over the canal, the Bourne, which we came to first, and the Sagamore, about five minutes farther on. Either one, obviously, will get you to the other side, but in the early years I thought I must take the Sagamore or I would surely end up in some alien spot on the Cape side and be lost. One year I remember, I headed up onto the Bourne Bridge while towing our small boat, the *Peteless*, then thought better of it and *backed* off, miraculously. It is maneuvers of this sort which makes Cape Codders believe that summer people are all crazy.

At any rate, we always used the Sagamore Bridge, even after we knew that either bridge would do. Tradition! I can hear Tevye in *Fiddler on the Roof* now. "Why do we do it? I'll tell you why. Tradition!"

A peak of excitement always occurred as our car descended the hump of the bridge and headed for the Cape side of the canal. At the precise moment of crossing this line

a chorus of voices screamed, "Cape Cod! Cape Cod!" We
had arrived again. Another year. All of us a year older, yet
not really, for wasn't everything the same as it was last year
—the canal, the mid-Cape highway, the scrubby pines, the
sandy soil, and the streams of traffic?

The cars going in our direction were called Happy People;
like us, they were heading for two weeks of fun. Cars coming
in the other direction, going off the Cape, were called Sad
People. Their vacation was over for another year. I used to
think that their station wagons and trailers and roof racks
were never as well or neatly packed as those on Happy
People's cars.

So it was that the canal had a great symbolic meaning for
our bunch—a frontier between mainland reality and the
mystic fantasy of the Cape. A moat, as it were, separating
schools and jobs and responsibilities and troubles from our
sandy makebelieveland, where fried clams and lobsters and
steamers awaited; where the waters of the bay were as warm
as a bath; where booming surf and low-tide flats and a white
cottage in the pines would make everything all right again.

Frankly, as many times as we crossed the canal, it never
really occurred to me that it wasn't put there just to be my
moat, that it had a real, if mundane, function and that real
people had something to do with running it. Real Cape Cod
people. They say there are some days in summer when
30,000 automobiles cross the canal. Do those people know
anything about the canal—or care? Who built it? Who uses
it? Who keeps it safe? Or is it just a moat to all summer

people? A pleasant, toll-free barrier to be crossed in a couple of minutes at forty miles an hour?

After fourteen summers, after all the Sad-Happy people were gone, I drove again to the canal. I was alone. The winds of winter were blowing now. Most of the gift shops along the route were closed. Motels had vacancy signs illuminated and notices about off-season rates being in effect. Fifty percent off, some of them said. The Leaning Tower of Pizza was closed. So was the Cranberry museum. It all seemed new and strange, like a theater after the show is over, like a stadium as the last spectators file out after the noise and color and excitement of the game.

I knew there must be someone in charge of the canal. For fourteen summers had I not read that sign: U.S. Army Corps of Engineers? Wouldn't it be an army base? I couldn't find one. I stopped at a gas station to ask directions.

"Just off that traffic circle and over the railroad bridge. It's a white house at the edge of the canal. You can't miss it." The universal words of reassurance to travelers, sometimes even true.

The building had a small porch facing the canal, with a front door in the middle of the porch. I went in and was greeted by a big cheerful man, middle-aged and a little gray. He was sitting at a desk by the front windows, facing the canal. From where he sat he could also look to the left, up toward Sandwich and Cape Cod Bay; to the right was Buzzard's Bay. On the desk were a radio set, a microphone, and a telephone. There was a big clock on the wall and some

radar equipment in back. The place looked like a dispatch-
er's office for a trucking company.

It was late in the afternoon. A winter sunset was just
beginning to turn the western sky slightly pink. Out in the
canal, ice chunks the size of tables and chairs were moving
swiftly by, bumping and crashing along from left to right,
east to west, in a constant flow. Unlike the summer scene
I remembered, there were no boats in sight.

"Lot of difference between summer and winter," the man
said. "Sometimes there's 200 small craft a day go through
the canal in summer, and on weekends we usually have to
tow four or five of 'em in. They have engine failures, lose
their rudders, that sort of thing."

His name was W. H. Chase, Jr. He was the Marine
Traffic Controller, a civilian who worked for the Corps of
Engineers. When he was on his eight-hour duty shift at that
desk, he ran the Cape Cod Canal.

"In the winter we don't have many small craft, but we still
have the tankers and freighters and some big tows—and we
have the ice. It's not that the canal ever gets completely
locked up, but if the ice is bad we may restrict traffic to one
way."

I told him I was interested in all this because I was writing
a book. I was really a summer person; I used to come often
to the Cape, I said, but usually in August.

"Summer people are perfectly welcome to stop in here
and visit. Sometimes they do." His accent was Massachusetts. "I call this canal a poor man's paradise for fishermen.

They don't need a license to fish here. In the summer we have a run of bluefish and striped bass. It's good fishing almost any time from April 15 to October 15. In the winter there's codfish and flounder. Course we don't allow fishing from boats, but along the banks is all right. There's a strip of federal land along both sides of the canal and about fourteen miles of service road that sportsmen are welcome to drive in with their cars or campers."

I asked if camping by the canal was allowed.

"Well," said Mr. Chase, "you know, if a fellow's in there fishing, our guards won't bother him. But if he seems to be sleeping, we might be obliged to ask him to move along."

They say Miles Standish was the first to propose a Cape Cod canal, in 1623; but no digging was ever done until 1880, when a company put 500 men to work with wheelbarrows. They didn't get far. Another try was made in 1899 and yet another in 1909. In July, 1914, a canal was finally cut through the same sandy valley it now occupies, but it was a shallow, narrow affair compared to the present waterway. The federal government finally enlarged the canal to its present 540-foot width and 32-foot depth in 1940.

"I can remember when it was a hundred feet or so wide and you could throw a baseball across it." Mr. Chase talked about his canal without ever taking his eyes off it. "I've been alongside this canal for fifty-three years now. You could say it's pretty much a part of my life. In 1934, when we had the WPA, I worked on those bridges, thirty hours a week."

Mr. Chase was born in Barnstable, which makes him a

true Cape Codder. I asked him how long he had been one of the traffic controllers.

"Let's see," he said, "twelve or thirteen years, I guess."

I wondered how many of those August days when we had crossed the bridge and whooped our ritual greetings to the Cape, Mr. W. H. Chase, Jr., had been right here in the white house I'd never seen before, taking care of the canal.

"We get about fifteen to seventeen big ships a day through here in the winter," he explained. "It saves them about five or six hours to come through the canal between Boston and New York—and it's a lot safer than going around the Cape and getting into those Nantucket Shoals. Besides, it's free. Doesn't cost anybody a cent to come through here, whether it's a kid's sailboat or a 700-foot tanker."

The radio on the desk in front of us came alive. I caught some words mixed with noise.

"*Effie Maersk* is coming through," Mr. Chase said, looking left. "She'll be along here any time now. That was my observer at the Sandwich end of the canal saying she'd entered."

He seemed to enjoy having company, but he said he didn't get lonely on the job as a rule. "There's always someone to talk to on the radio," he explained, "even at night."

I watched the canal flowing by, looking the way I had always imagined the ice-choked river in *Uncle Tom's Cabin*. It occurred to me that I had never actually seen it move before, one way or the other. From the Sagamore Bridge in

August it was simply a stationary blue ribbon below. I wondered now if it always flowed from the Cape's big inner bay out to Buzzard's Bay at the southwest. Mr. Chase chuckled at my question. Summer people sure don't know much, I suppose he thought.

"She runs six hours in one direction, then turns and runs six hours in the other. Goes four ways every day." I could see that a five-knot current, full of ice floes, was pretty treacherous no matter which way it flowed.

"Oh, we've had 'em go aground in here," Mr. Chase said. "Their engine strainers get clogged with ice and they have an engine failure and then they drift onto a shoal. That's why we keep these two tugs here, for emergencies." The tugs are berthed right next to the headquarters building.

I could see a big blue-hulled freighter coming from the left, looking huge and high in the water as it passed between the canal banks.

"There's the *Maersk*," said Mr. Chase, picking up his microphone. He exchanged a few words with the vessel's pilot on the bridge, telling him to watch out for a Coast Guard buoy tender working near the western end of the canal. A friendly "Roger" came back from the *Maersk* as she slid by with the current, making no sound and leaving no wake in the ice floes.

"They usually pass through here just like that," Mr. Chase said. "No problems. But you've got to have a feel for the weather. Running with the tide, it takes a ship about an hour and twenty minutes to transit the canal, or two hours against the current. Trouble is, we can have a vapor rise in here so you can't see the opposite bank in fifteen minutes. They call this Fog Corners."

It was getting darker now as we talked. Lights came on along the canal banks.

"They're mercury lights—one every 500 feet," Mr. Chase said. "In the summer, of course, we have the lighted channel markers too, but they get pulled under the ice in the winter, so we replace them with marker cans. And they get pulled under too, so there can be hazards in here at night."

He looked straight ahead through the window. "She's an island over there. Not many people realize it, but Cape Cod is an island. Because of this canal."

I admitted I'd never really thought of it that way.

"She's an island, all right," said Mr. Chase.

There seemed to be a certain finality to that thought. I got up to say goodbye.

"Come by again," Mr. Chase said sincerely. "Come by anytime. Don't wait till next summer. We're always here."

THE ELECTRIC
TRAIN MAN

In summer, there was a place called the Eastham Country Store and Campground on Route 6. It was a small, building with some windows and a screen door at the front and a loop of blacktop driveway leading in and out to the highway. Usually an American flag was flying from a pole by the door, and a Sunbeam Bread sign stood between the driveway and the road. Behind the main building a few small summer cottages seemed to lurk under trees. Sometimes the proprietor put plastic floats and beachballs outside the store to indicate, I suppose, that he sold plastic floats and beachballs.

This store was always open early on August mornings. If we were out of milk or bread or wanted a paper, we would stop there on our way back from the Doughnut Shack. The car would be full of the rich brown scent of fresh doughnuts, still warm in their white paper bag. Glazed doughnuts, looking slightly deflated, their crystalline skins wrinkled and cracked. Cinnamon doughnuts, firmer and dryer. Jelly doughnuts with little bleeding navels. Get blueberry, Dad. Or raspberry. *No* lemon ones, Dad! Three of each. Four! Then who would carry the precious selection on the way back to breakfast? Oldest Jenny? Sister Becky? Son Chuck? Little Patrick? Whoever, the day's custodian got to hold the warm bag on his lap and stuff his nose into the top and make immediate plans. . . .

When we stopped at the store I would ask if we needed anything besides the milk and paper. Kite string? Beach-plum jelly? Another one of those balsawood gliders?

The fellow who ran the place was about my age, tall and lean, and he moved slowly and quietly behind the counters like a man wearing soft moccasins. He spoke with a New England accent, but it wasn't exactly Cape Cod. I could not quite place it.

"Mornin'," he'd say.

"Think it will rain?" I'd ask.

"Might," he'd say.

Summer people always want to know if it's going to rain. If they had their collective way, not a drop of moisture would fall on the Cape from June to September.

The store was a curious little place, never very well lighted, never crowded, its shelves containing what seemed only a few days' supply of simple needs: a few boxes of dry cereal, some pancake flour, bottles of maple syrup, soap and toothpaste, paper plates and napkins, suntan oil and bug spray, toys for the beach, including kites, shovels, small plastic boats, and sand pails. But in a glass case at the rear of the store was the most interesting display of all—a small collection of old electric trains. Lionel, Ives, American Flyer. I never bought anything there without stopping a moment to look at the trains. They brought back memories of the thirties: the Hiawatha, the Twentieth Century Limited, flickering bulbs inside passenger coaches.

"Didn't you say you had one just like that, Dad?" one of the kids would ask each year.

"Just like that black one," I'd say.

"One like that?" the man would ask, appearing from behind the counter. "I'll buy it from you anytime you're ready to sell."

"No thanks," I'd say, "but I like your collection. Are any of them for sale?"

"Not for sale," he'd say.

We bought things in that store for eight or ten years. I noticed that the collection of trains grew a little each year. But I never knew why the man displayed them right along with the bread and the canned goods and the boxes of soap powder. As a matter of fact, I never learned his name; we just used to call him the Electric Train Man.

"Ed Putnam's my name," he told me one day last winter. "I think I remember you. You were here a good many summers, weren't you?"

Yes, I said, a good many summers. And now I was trying

to find out what the winter was like. Don't ask me why, Mr. Putnam. I'll find out later, maybe. Right now, I said, I was writing a book about Cape Cod in the winter—going back over old trails, I thought, fitting my shoes into the footprints, so to speak, saying to myself, "Yes, here is where we walked. I can still see the tracks. They aren't gone yet. . . ."

The store had changed. There were no more groceries, no more household supplies, no newspapers, none of summer's brown children—only trains. Trains everywhere. Every shelf, table, and counter was full of them. Antique trains and new trains. Big old standard-gauge steamers and tiny scale models.

"What happened to all the groceries?" I asked.

"I gave up the groceries," said Mr. Putnam. I still could not pin down his accent. "The store's gone back to what I really like to do, which is to sell trains."

Along one wall, a waist-high platform had been built for a complicated track layout. Several old trains sat on sidings. There were bridges and tunnels and stations and crossing gates and wires going in every direction, and switches and transformers and semaphores and a big open space at the center so the operators could crawl under and come right up into the middle of the whole layout.

"I'm an official Lionel dealer now," Mr. Putnam explained with a certain pride as we walked around the store. It was February and there were no other customers. A storm the week before had left the roads still lined with plowed-up piles of sandy-brown snow. There wasn't much traffic on Route 6. "This is the only train store south of Boston," Mr. Putnam said. "People come here from all over."

I asked if he sold or traded the old trains now.

"Oh, no. I just sell the new stuff. I've been collecting tin plate for twenty-five years, but it's not for sale. I'm only a buyer. It's getting pretty scarce, though. The good stuff, that is. Sometimes I'll go as far as Cheshire and New Haven to look at trains. Course there's a lot of junk around."

I said I'd heard that some of the old trains—the fans call them tin plate—were worth a lot of money to collectors. Mr. Putnam looked at me a little suspiciously.

"We don't want people to know what this stuff is worth," he said. "It just gives someone who has an old train the idea that it's priceless when the damn thing probably isn't worth twenty dollars. Then you try to buy it from them and they want a hundred and twenty." This was obviously a subject on which Mr. Putnam had strong feelings.

"See that Hellgate Bridge over there?" It was a big one, a replica of the famous railroad bridge into New York City. I remembered it from my old Lionel catalog of the thirties. "It's worth $75 today. But it's the only one of the bridges that's worth anything. All those others, they made 'em by the millions. Not worth a cent.

"Did you look at that maroon train set there on the middle shelf? I got that one from an old man about seventy-five up in Northampton. He had it new. That's the first electric Lionel ever made. 1911."

Mr. Putnam's accent was still puzzling me. "How long have you lived on the Cape, Mr. Putnam?" I asked.

"I've been living here year round for about ten years, but my wife and I used to come here summers long before that. I'm not a Cape Codder. I'm a Vermonter." There it was, the hillsong of Vermont. Sweet. Precise. "I owned a TV and appliance business in Brattleboro. Sold out. Moved down here because we liked it. Warmer in the winters. Ten degrees warmer than Boston or even down south in Connecticut. I'm an awful Vermonter. I hate snow." Laugh. Who ever heard of such a thing?

"But this is the worst winter I've ever seen here on the Cape. Worst in thirty years, they tell me. Pipes freezing in cottages all over."

Tell that to all those summer people who have been told it never snows or even freezes on the Cape. The legend of the Cape's balmy winters is repeated and believed from year to year by the July-and-August folk. If you told them palm trees grow in Hyannis they might even believe it.

"Did you know you've come to a historic spot?" Mr. Putnam asked.

I thought of Indian encounters. Pilgrim explorations. Ship sinkings. Marconi's wireless experiments. I gave up.

"This place is the site of the first campground on the Cape," Mr. Putnam explained. "1927. The cottages and the campground are out back. I've got two families who come every summer whose fathers came here in 1927. Course you get all kinds now. Camping's getting big. They come in here even on winter days like this and want to know if they can camp or rent a cottage. I tell 'em no. Cottages are closed until April."

I wondered what kind of people went camping in the winter.

"Fishermen. And surfers. But I don't take those. I take only families. Surfers . . ." he shook his head, "that's a different generation to me. I can't handle several generations in here. So I *discriminate* something fierce. It's a family place and it's going to stay that way."

Together, we looked out the window of the front door at the gray afternoon and the slush. "I'll predict something," said Mr. Putnam. "Within another seven to ten years, the Cape is going to be a big winter place for people who don't ski."

Would that be good for the train business, I wanted to know.

"Can't tell. The train business goes in cycles. Ten years ago, I couldn't give a train set away. Everybody said slot cars were going to replace the trains. But the trains came back. They always will. I remember what a big thing it was in the thirties. Then it died down, now it's back again.

"Last fall was pretty heavy. People came down here from everywhere to check their cottages as late as November. Then they stop in here and maybe buy a $50 engine or $70 worth of parts. That's the way it goes.

"In October and until after Christmas, the tin plate collectors come by. We've got 2500 members across the country now, and they look in the directory and they say, 'There's Putnam down on Cape Cod. Let's go see him.' They come in here, and we talk trains and compare notes. I don't have time to do that in the summer, of course, and that's one reason I like the winter better.

"Then we have our open-house parties here on Sunday afternoons in November and December. Everybody on the Cape brings their children. We run all those old trains on those tracks you see there, noon to six o'clock. We pour out cranberry juice for them, and it takes three of us just to keep things going. Jesus, by the time Christmas is over, we are sick of running those trains, I tell you. But it sure brings business into the place. It works out real good.

"February's hard scratching, though. There's no money coming in around here in February. I'm about down to the bottom of the barrel right now. But it always works out somehow. I start getting deposits on the cottages and camp-sites for next summer about now, and that keeps me going. You see, the trains are just a hobby that has turned into a business. You don't get rich at it, but it beats living in the city and fighting the pollution."

I agreed with him on that.

"There's also some money in train repairs that helps me buy groceries in the winter. I tell people that some good old engines are worth $25 or $30 to repair. But if it's junk, I just tell 'em it isn't worth fixing. You've got to be honest, you know." Mr. Putnam's face was long and serious.

"I've got $500 tied up just in Lionel repair manuals.

Don't work by the hour or anything like that, though. I just charge what I think a job is worth."

We were in a back room now, wandering around. The repair bench was cluttered with bits and pieces of trains. The room itself was lined with shelves from floor to ceiling, all of them full of train sets: passenger trains, freight sets, floodlight cars, cranes. I remembered them all.

"Why do you keep collecting?" I asked.

"Oh, it gets in your blood, I guess. I'm going to pass it all along to my son. It'll be worth something to him someday."

I thought of my boys and how they liked the trains.

"What's it all worth?" I asked.

"Oh, I couldn't give you a figure," said Mr. Putnam with the kindly smile of a Vermont horse trader. "I wouldn't tell you. It's more than I want to mention."

He said he worried about robbery. "They hit the cottages around here pretty regular now in the winter. Any place that's a little isolated. It's a big worry to me. Not that anyone would want much of this stuff. They'd have no idea what to do with it anyway."

Mr. Putnam picked up a freight car from the workbench and fitted a pair of wheels where they belonged.

"I'm as small an operator as you'll find. A real one-man business. I don't make much money, but I have a lot of fun."

I told him I'd come by again sometime when I was passing through Eastham.

"Come any time," he said. "Next time, bring the kids."

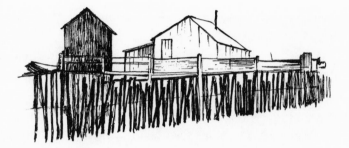

FISH HATCHERY

As summer people, we did what many July-and-August folk
do, exploring the Cape's byways and secondary roads, pros-
pecting in both directions from our base in Eastham, as the
1620 Pilgrims had done both on foot and by water to dis-
cover more about this spit of sand on which they had landed.
A rainy day was usually a good time to get into the car and
wander (which is one reason the Cape has traffic jams on
rainy days in summer!) No place seems too distant from
another on Cape Cod, but for the most part it was the lower
Cape, that narrow land from the elbow to the fist, that
intrigued us most. As a result, whatever went on on the
upper Cape, between the canal and Chatham, was largely
unknown to us. Booming, overdeveloped Hyannis seemed a
place to avoid; Falmouth was far away indeed. The heart-
land around Otis Air Force Base was entirely mysterious.
And fine, famous old towns like Sandwich were always

"someplace we should really go see some day." We never did.

It was on a January day much later that I was driving along Route 6A in Sandwich. The temperature was above freezing, but the winter sun was as flat and cold as an aluminum pie plate. Traffic was sparse on the old, narrow blacktop road. The Cape Cod houses—the cottages under their big, steep roofs, the asymmetrical salt boxes, the four-square old Colonials with white clapboards and many windows—all seemed etched in sharp outline against the clean air. The ancient elms, so green and graceful along summer's roadsides, were now drawn in crisp, black lines on the cold blue sky.

Just outside of town my eye spotted a sign that said, "Commonwealth of Massachusetts, Division of Fisheries and Game, Sandwich Fish Hatchery, Open 9 A.M. to 4 P.M." There was an entrance in a tall fence and a driveway leading between two rows of towering evergreens. It was nearly four, but I decided to go in and have a look.

At first glance the fish hatchery didn't look like much: an administration building, a long, low cinder-block building, and a large number of deep rectangular concrete pools set flush in the ground. I parked and began to wander about. The first pools I came to were about twenty-five feet long, six feet wide, and three or four feet deep, and in the dark, clean water dozens of giant old trout cruised like prowling submarines. There seemed to be all kinds—browns, rainbows, and brookies. Attached to a pole near the first pool was a machine that dispensed a handful of green pellets for a dime. I bought some of the food and tossed a few bits toward the fish. The surface of the water erupted with frantic thrashings, and the pellets disappeared. I thought these fish must be pretty well fed by summer visitors, but treats from the pellet machine were probably few and far between in winter. No other car but mine was in sight, and no other visitors.

I headed for the long, low building, where I saw a man carrying a bucket. He went over to one of the pools and began ladling great slops of red liquid into the water, his arm moving in a wide arc each time and the ladle spewing what looked like blood in long streams through the air. Soon he emptied the bucket and went back toward the building. I was waiting for him at the door.

"You keep that busy all winter?" I asked.

"Yessir," he said, "we have to feed those small ones every day this time of year." He was a young man, dark skinned, good looking, and ramrod straight.

I introduced myself. He said his name was Larry Hollings. From Mashpee. I thought he might be an Indian descendant, but I didn't think to ask.

"What goes on around here in the winter?" I asked.

"Winter's the busiest time in some ways," Mr. Hollings replied. "Summer's pretty quiet far as the fish are concerned. Course we have lots of visitors here—thirty or forty cars sometimes in the parking lot—but things don't really get interesting until late fall when we take the eggs from the females."

Together we stepped into the building. Inside, it resembled a dairy shed. A big pump was running somewhere, making a lot of noise. I asked Mr. Hollings what happened with the eggs.

"Well, it's the same as with salmon. We squeeze the eggs and the sperm from our brood stock and we set 'em out in these long trays here to hatch. This is usually in October. Takes thirty-five days. We keep the fry in here for about a week before we put 'em out in the pools." Mr. Hollings was friendly and expert with his answers. I asked him how such small fish could survive the winter.

"We put 'em out there in December, usually. Actually, the water has to be cold for the eggs and the little ones— 45 degrees is about right. You see, our water never freezes in the pools because it comes out of deep wells. Comes up at about 48 degrees and keeps moving."

What was that stuff he was feeding the fish, I asked.

"That's Grade-A beef liver," said Mr. Hollings, moving over to refill his bucket. "It's edible liver. We get it from a mink farm in Michigan. They need fish to feed the mink, so they send trucks out here to the Cape to buy all kinds of trash fish at Provincetown and instead of sending 'em empty, they sell us this midwest beef liver. Makes a nice arrangement."

He scooped up enough of the ground liver slop to fill his pail again. "It has to be ground fine," Mr. Hollings explained, "especially for the little ones. When we first put 'em out there in December, we have to feed 'em once an *hour*. If they don't learn to eat in the first two or three weeks, that's the end of 'em. They just die."

We walked out to one of the pools, where the youngest fish were kept. This was shallower than the pools where the old brood stock lived. Thousands, tens of thousands, maybe hundreds of thousands of tiny trout, about a half-inch long now, swarmed in the pool. Wherever Mr. Hollings tossed in a ladleful of bloody liver, the fish rushed like iron filings to a magnet.

"I feed ten pounds of liver six times a day in a pool like this," he said.

"How many make it through the winter?" I asked.

"We have about 70 to 80 percent survival in the hatchery," Mr. Hollings said with a touch of pride. "That's a lot better than nature does. If 3 percent survive in the wild, that's average. Some years we put out four or five million fish. Lately we've been releasing about 140,000 pounds of live fish into public waters every April."

I asked where he'd gotten his training. His explanations were scientific and informed.

"I learned the hard way," Mr. Hollings said with a smile. "Right from scratch, right here at the hatchery. Been here sixteen years, except for the time I spent as an instructor in the Marines at Parris Island." That explained his straight posture.

"Do you ever take a trout home to dinner?" I asked, somewhat in fun.

He looked at me seriously. "Oh, no. I do my own fishing in season. Besides, you know, these fish don't taste good. They taste like liver. Takes almost three weeks of living in the wild for 'em to lose that taste."

I thanked Mr. Hollings for the time he'd spent with me.

"Not at all. A pleasure. Come anytime. We like to have people come in, especially with children. If they come in a group, we'll explain things to them. Too bad more of 'em can't come in the winter, though. That's when it's really interesting."

DOLPHINS
IN DECEMBER

I REMEMBER seeing a gunfight on Cape Cod one summer.
Right in the middle of a dusty town with a sandy main
street. It was make-believe, of course, a fake gunfight between a sheriff and a bad guy named Black Bart, staged in
front of an old western-style saloon at a false-front amusement center called Kiddieland or some such name. The
sheriff had a dreadful Massachusetts accent which didn't go
with his western clothes, but when he called on "Black
Baht" to draw, Jenny and Becky stood tense and breathless
in their little red sunsuits, waiting to hear the guns go off.

There was also a magician called Kevin the Konjurer.
(Why have these names kept so long?) Kevin was young,
Boston Irish, and clever with his hands. He had Chuck
completely baffled by the old illusion of the Multiplying
Billiard Balls.

I also remember pony rides; a big concrete Mother Goose with a mouse that ran up a concrete clock; and the cool, dark interior of the aquarium at Provincetown, where the kids tentatively put their fingers on the glass until a large, black ray stirred into threatening movement, like a living rug shaking itself.

The Cape was never what one would call an amusement park, but it had amusements of this sort, and the kids always remembered them. Like most summer people, however, we never stopped to wonder who Black Baht really was, or whether the fish stayed in the Provincetown aquarium all winter. Cape Cod was all one big show; we knew the curtain went up in July and came down after Labor Day. What happened to the actors after that was never a matter of interest.

Last winter I met four of summer's actors swimming in a large concrete pool in Brewster. Although there was snow on the ground, and the temperature was in the thirties, these characters were cavorting in 70-degree comfort. Their names were Salty, Stormy, Spray, and Sergeant. They were dolphins.

Sealand, on Route 6A, isn't strictly for amusement. A man named Bob King has been running it for six years now, putting a lot of emphasis on educational projects, but there can be no denying the entertainment value in performing dolphins.

Mr. King welcomed me one dreary afternoon. His parking lot was empty, but the front door to Sealand's main building was open.

"Come on in," he said, "I'm just doing the dishes. Can I get you a cup of coffee?"

I explained that I hadn't come to see the show, just to find out more about people who kept open all winter on the Cape. Why did he do it?

"We don't have a lot of choice. We have to keep the dolphins here, have to feed them. Costs too much to move dolphins around from one place to another." Mr. King is a friendly, middle-aged man. He led me into a back room, a combination office, workshop, kitchenette, and den, where there were several tanks of fish and pumps circulating water. The dolphins were housed in a separate building.

"What made you get into show business?" I asked.

Pause.

"Isn't this show business in a way?" I said, noting that Mr. King wasn't answering me. When he did, he spoke very slowly.

"Well, in a way, yes. But we'd like to think it's more educational. We have twenty to thirty thousand children a year who come here in groups with their teachers. Keeps us pretty busy from September right through June. We're the only educational institution of its kind in this part of New England. We even have kids come here from Rhode Island and Connecticut."

A younger man, who introduced himself as Karel B. Zielinski, Jr., came in the back door. Mr. King said Karel was his educational director, a former school teacher from Great Barrington, Mass.

"How do you like the Cape in the winter?" I asked him.

"It's rotten, if you want to know the truth," said young Mr. Zielinski with a good-natured laugh. Then he added, "Especially if you're single like me."

I asked him about his educational program.

"We try to emphasize that a dolphin is a highly intelligent mammal that is capable of far more than tricks in a show. We also give out a little scholarship money to students who are studying marine biology, that sort of thing, and we have a consulting service with teachers. Keeps us busy. We're much busier in the winter than in the summer, I'd say."

In summer Sealand does five scheduled shows a day. "We're usually packed," Mr. King said. "Then when winter comes, we schedule three shows a day, though we usually do just one. But even if only one person shows up and pays his admission, he gets a show."

Could we take a look at the dolphins, I asked? Both men seemed anxious to show off the pets. We went out the back door, across the snowy yard, and into a much bigger building which housed the pool. Inside, it was warm and humid. Dolphin squeaks filled the air. Mr. King flipped on some lights.

"We keep it 70 degrees in here, winter and summer. The water is 70 and the air is 70." Out of the dark water boiled the big, arched back of a dolphin. The hide was vinyl shiny. Two more shapes cruised just under the surface.

"They've been asleep on the bottom," said Mr. Zielinski. He shouted at the dolphins, calling them by name: "Salty!

Stormy! Sergeant! Spray!" Then they came to him, lifting their heads out of the water, chirping, huffing, and puffing wetly through the blowholes on their heads.

"Spray there was a back-up dolphin at the New York World's Fair. She knows at least fifty words of English." Both men leaned over the rail of the pool and talked to the creatures like old friends.

In summers past I had seen dolphins off the Cape beaches a few times. I asked if these four were natives.

"No," said Mr. King, "they're from Florida. Several types of dolphins sometimes come as far north in the summer as the Cape. There's about six varieties found in the bay, but they aren't as limber as these southern dolphins and can't do as many tricks."

I wondered what a dolphin from Florida cost.

"An untrained dolphin costs about $500 in Florida, plus shipping charges. They just put them in a big box and they go right into the cargo hold of a passenger plane," Mr. King explained. "A dolphin can live about a week out of water."

The dolphins were playing with a beach ball now, shoving it around on their noses and bringing it to Mr. Zielinski to play. I wondered how often they were fed.

"Once a day is enough," said Mr. Zielinski. "They'll eat 17 to 20 pounds of fish a day. We keep 10,000 pounds of frozen fish in stock—hake and herring mostly—a dry fish and an oily fish for a balanced diet. You could eat it yourself. The hake is the same fish they use around here for fish chowder."

"Are they happy like this?" I asked. "Spending their lives in this concrete pool?"

"Oh, definitely," said Mr. Zielinski. "They like it here."

Did he ever want to jump in and go for a swim with them, I wondered.

"Had a swim with 'em this morning," he answered with a laugh. "Pretty nice, middle of winter."

Cold New England air cut through my clothes when we came out of the warm humidity of the dolphins' world. Summer seemed far away, now. There were no other visitors at Sealand, no traffic on the road. I thanked my friends for showing me around.

"Come again," said Mr. King. "We're always here—like farmers."

WINTER SANCTUARY

PRISCILLA BAILEY knows that winter is on its way to the Cape when she sees the eiders and scoters come in from the north in November and begin feeding on the mussels in her salt marsh.

"But it's nothing we dread," she says. "We like the winter here. It's a time to rest."

Mrs. Bailey's husband Wallace is the resident director of the Audubon Society's big bird sanctuary in Wellfleet. They live in a century-old house—actually two old farmhouses which were joined—on a 600-acre tract that is two-thirds salt marsh. The sanctuary is a mecca for "birders" from all over New England.

I dropped in on her one day in early March. It was gray and cold that day, as it had been the only other time I had visited the sanctuary—but that had been in summer.

A northeast storm is the worst kind you can get in New

England, winter or summer. A northeaster in August can last three or four days, and nothing is more difficult for summer people to endure than several consecutive days of rain, fog, low clouds racing by, cool wind, and everything hanging wet on the clothes line. After the first day or so, children become impatient and irritable, and parents search desperately for some activity to replace the long lazy hours on the beach. It was during just such a spell many years ago that we turned to Audubon for help.

"Come on, kids," I said, "let's go see some birds," and off we went until we found the sign along Route 6 and turned onto a narrow road through a dense stand of scrub pine.

Then and now, the sanctuary is a deceptive place. You see first just the old residence with a friendly-looking screened front porch; an inner door leads to a small reception room with spartan furnishings and a glass case full of stuffed birds against one wall. A sort of picnic area is arranged under a tall stand of pines near the ample parking lot, and a trail with some markers leads away toward the marshland. Here and there you can see bird houses on tall poles and feeding stations.

"Some people are disappointed," Mrs. Bailey told me. "They come in and ask where the birds are. I think they expect to find them in big cages, like a zoo. When we explain that it isn't that way, they get in their car and go away."

I remembered having the same feeling. Somehow, I thought a bird sanctuary would be a place where birds by the thousands had been lured by free food and guaranteed security. On that day long ago, as we walked along the trails, looking hopefully at the sky for some sign that the sun would come out, the kids had grumbled. "I thought you said there would be birds, Dad?" Very few were in sight. Some days a parent can't do anything right.

"We get some summer people who complain to us that the trails are muddy and should be paved, or that the mosquitos are bad in the woods and why don't we spray?" Mrs. Bailey is a mild and pleasant lady. She just added, "Summer people are funny."

As for the number of birds in the sanctuary, she said there were probably no more within the Audubon boundaries than in the surrounding area. "In the winter we put some corn out in the marsh for a few birds that are almost tame —blacks, mallards, and Canada geese—but our purpose here isn't so much to feed as it is to preserve the habitat. Of course, we don't use any insecticides, so maybe there are more bugs for the birds to eat in the summer."

I explained that I was particularly interested in winter on the Cape. Were there visitors at the sanctuary year round?

"On a good weekend in winter there will be ten or twelve cars in the parking lot sometimes. There are a different type, the winter people. They usually know what they're looking for and why they're here. They don't ask for any help. Some may even want to rent one of the three unheated cottages that we open in the summer. They're people who have read Beston and Thoreau and want to participate in a similar experience themselves. Many of them are young, and it pleases us to see that.

"In the summer months we have about 50,000 visitors. During the other ten months of the year, we have about 10,000. It's a good thing winter comes, we think. If we had the summer crowds year round, there wouldn't be a bird to look at in here. Winter's the time for the land and . . ." Mrs. Bailey laughed, "the *staff* to recover! Not that there's any shortage of things to do in winter," she added. "Wallace is busy all the time with maintenance.

"Last winter was a hard one," she said, looking out the window at the slate-colored sky. The marsh was full of ice and the water birds had a hard time—the salt-water ducks and the loons and some of the land birds who usually stay with us all winter. But it's about over now," Mrs. Bailey added with a smile.

"How do you know when spring is really here," I asked.

"Oh, the day we see the first singing redwing," she said happily. "This year it was February 26. We posted the date on that sign by the door so visitors would know."

Were there other sure signs that winter was over?

"When the piping plovers come to the outer beaches in mid-March usually. It's not long after that that things begin to stir."

I thanked her for our talk.

"Are you a birder?" she asked as I was leaving.

"No," I said, "I don't know much about birds."

"Well, come again anyway," she said. "This is a nice place just to walk, summer or winter."

HAUNTED HOUSES

One thing we used to like to do for a diversion on summer days was to explore what the kids called haunted houses— old abandoned places that we sometimes found along the back roads. Sometimes it was a summer cottage, clearly deserted, or an old farmhouse with windows and doors smashed in, or some Victorian skeleton abandoned to the elements. I don't mean that such derelict structures are a common sight on Cape Cod; to the contrary, the Cape is a place where old houses are more often preserved than neglected. Perhaps that's what made our occasional discoveries all the more exciting.

The first obligation, of course, was to be sure that the object of our curiosity and explorer instincts was truly abandoned and not just someone's temporarily unoccupied summer place. This required a parent to be cautious at times.

"Come on, Dad, it's empty!" Chuck might shout when

we found some tempting old structure—and just then I would see the dishtowels and bathing suits hanging on a backyard clothesline.

In most cases, however, a truly abandoned house is self-evident. It has a quality about it as fascinating to me as it was to the children: forlorn, yet somehow proud, as if to say, "Here I still stand, and although my windows and shingles may be shattered and weathered, I have strong old bones."

Sometimes, as we reconnoitered, we would try to recon-struct a story about the house, try to picture the people who must have lived there, try to understand what had happened to them, where they had gone and why. A haunted house was never just a house, after all. There were always other artifacts scattered about, nothing of any use or value, but human signs all the same. Old mattresses, broken dishes, a refrigerator with the door removed, an old bathtub, narrow and deep, standing on four cast-iron claw feet. Sometimes the wallpaper said this was a child's room. Sometimes a calendar on the wall gave some clue as to when the last occupants had lived there. Or a cupboard full of glass jars and paraffin caps said that the lady of the house had proba-bly made beach-plum jelly.

It was a rule that we would enter only if the door was open, or, as was often the case, missing altogether. Then, like scouts, we would scatter through the old rooms, and there would be cries of, "Hey, look at this!" or, "This place must have been empty for years!" If a door slammed shut behind our backs, or a loose brick fell down a chimney into a fireplace, or an old window sash dropped with a crash of glass, we jumped a mile. Such scares had a delicious quality that confirmed the mysterious dangers of exploring a haunted house and made summer sunshine feel strong and good when we finally emerged from what seemed like the cool of an old tomb. Outside again, the smell of dead, damp plaster was replaced with the sweet, salt-scented air of the Cape.

If the houses we found were often askew, with the porch roof sagging or the chimney leaning like an old man about to lose his balance, the living things around them seemed to prosper without regard for time. Lilacs planted at the kitchen door by some long-ago Cape Codder would be a towering thicket of healthy green, and iris, oblivious to neglect and indifferent to abandonment, often spread green spears along a cellar wall or still marked the border of a walk.

"Look out for that poison ivy," I would sometimes warn the little ones. The roots of this beautiful, strong plant with the simonized leaves spread deep in the Cape's sandy soil, and its centipede-like tendrils hold to the silvered shingles of an abandoned house as if to say, "Now it is mine. . . ."

Once an exploration was complete, we would often stand back from our new trophy, appraising it as a whole, seeing how it set with the land, and one of the kids would always say, "Let's buy it, Dad, and fix it up. . . ."

Each and every one of the many old houses that formed our personal collection was considered a candidate for a complete restoration job. The thought was always, somehow, to preserve, never to tear down. Even when common sense told us that rotten wood cannot be saved, that antique plumbing is worthless, that electricians are expensive, we nevertheless enjoyed our fantasies.

"Bet we could buy it cheap, Dad. Let's find out who owns it, Dad! Come on, Dad!"

From year to year we would watch these houses, often going out of our way to see if one of the old friends was still standing, or whether some shrewd summer people with more money than we had bought *our* place out from under *our* noses.

Over the many summers, the houses did disappear, one by one. Fire took several of them, not surprisingly, and the wreckers disposed of others as land to build on became more and more sought after. But it was always the houses that were bought by some apparently farsighted and courageous investor and then restored which aroused a sort of bitter-sweet pride and envy in our hearts. It was, after all, our house before it was theirs. We knew it before they did. We had loved it first and had seen its possibilities. Sometimes we were critical of what the new owners had done.

"Look, they cut down that big tree!" one of us would say, with a note of bitterness. Huns.

"Place doesn't look right without the old barn in back." Insensitive barbarians.

"Now what did they have to go and tear the nice old porch off for?" New Yorkers.

Of all the haunted houses we explored, there was one we always remembered best.

"That's where Becky found the big candle, isn't it?" Chuck would say years later.

"And there was an outhouse out back. . . ."

There was. Two rows of neat, round holes carved in plank seats, the whole place whitewashed on the inside. By the time we discovered it, it was home to a frightening squadron of wasps, and the trellis was covered by an impenetrable growth of honeysuckle. The main building was, even in its shabby state, still sound: a big strong barnlike structure with a steep roof. It could have been a church or a meeting house or even an abandoned fire station for all we knew, until we stepped in through the back door and saw the blackboards around all the walls. Obviously, it had been a one-room school—and something else, too, because people had been living in it.

The schoolhouse isn't far from the center of Eastham, just off Route 6 and now just across from the new National Park and Seashore Visitors' Center. There was nothing particularly secret about it or spooky either, but once inside we felt like visitors in a lost world, a place where Cape Cod children had once sat at tiny maple desks with cast-iron legs and where, later, some family had kept warm in winter around the giant old wood stove. Becky's candle, a pound or two of old discolored wax, was the single souvenir we took away.

"We paid $7500 for that schoolhouse," Fred Jewell told me last winter. "Didn't know whether we could ever fix it up or not. All sorts of people had lived there after it was a school and it sure was a mess inside."

I agreed that it was.

"Did you see it years ago?" Mr. Jewell is retired, vigorous, opinionated, a bundle of energy with a penetrating voice.

Yes, years ago, I said, remembering the mess and the blackboards and the wasps and the desks. It's all changed now, transformed in the last few years into a handsome little museum and headquarters for the Eastham Historical Society, Mr. Frederick H. Jewell, founder, curator, archivist, contract printer, public-relations director, and prime mover. It was good to see that one of our haunted houses had been turned to such good use.

The old schoolhouse contains a great collection of Cape Cod memorabilia. Old furniture, tools, photographs, harpoons, a section of wooden water pipe, some of the old school desks, scrimshaw, old maps, the skeletal remains of some Nauset Indians, some jewelry and eyeglass frames, old paintings, and prints.

I first met Fred Jewell one early spring day over near the herring run that leads into one of Eastham's many fresh water ponds. It wasn't the sort of day when many people were abroad, but I saw this busy figure of a man watering some young pine seedlings that had just been planted, and I decided to have a talk.

"Your name's Barnard?" he said, full of immediate curiosity. "We've got Barnards living here in Eastham."

I said I knew Bruce Barnard on Meetinghouse Road. He had been a summer friend of my children.

"Then you're no kin?" No kin, I said. Just a coincidence.

"We put out 5000 of these seedlings this spring," Mr. Jewell said. "More than any other town on the Cape. Black pine, Scotch pine, autumn olive. Some roses, too. Summer people order them and come up here early spring and plant them on their property. It's just one of many projects I fool around with."

When I came back months later to visit with Mr. and Mrs. Jewell at home, I found two retired people who had seen much of the world and were now happy to pour all their considerable energies into Eastham, Massachusetts. Summer and winter.

"Nobody does anything here in the summer except make money off the tourists. Lot of people have two jobs in the summer. Life is a lot more satisfying in the winter. I'd say the best weather is from the middle of September to Thanksgiving. After that you can get what we call the Montreal Express—a northwest wind out of Canada. When that comes, it blows right through the place, and we take our meals right here in front of the fireplace."

The Jewells' house is a rambling, century-old structure with small cozy rooms. Two great camphorwood chests with ornate brass corners and bindings announce that the people who live here probably know something about Orient.

"I was with the British-American Tobacco Company," Mr. Jewell said after I'd remarked about the chests. "We had manufacturing facilities in Shanghai, Harbin, and

Tientsin. Lived in China from 1921 to 1928. Imported cigarettes from England and Egypt and cigars from Jamaica and we made some cheap local brands in Shanghai. One of them was called Ruby Queen in a pink package, ten cigarettes. Cost about two or three cents in our money. . . ." Once Mr. Jewell began to review his days in the Orient there was no stopping him.

"Then from 1928 to 1938, we traveled all over Japan and the Philippines and Malaya selling Enos Salts, Keating's Powder, Cold Tar Soap, Scott's Emulsion, and marmalade.

"Lived in Connecticut from 1938 to 1943, then went to the West Indies and South America as a sales representative for another tobacco company. . . .

"Lived in Dobbs Ferry from 1948 to 1955 . . ." I finally succeeded in breaking in with a question. When did he first come to Cape Cod?

"Cape Cod?" Mr. Jewell's voice rose. "I never heard of Cape Cod! I'm a Middlewesterner, born and raised in Iowa and Illinois! Cape Cod meant nothing to me! The first time I came out here it was just for a drive, and I didn't think much of the place. We had a flat tire in Dennis so we turned around, and I didn't care if I never saw Cape Cod again."

They bought their house in Eastham in 1952.

"We drove out here for a few days, picked up a real-estate man, and started looking around. It was getting dark when we drove in the back yard of this place, but we liked what we saw so we gave the agent $100 in traveler's checks and that was it."

Mr. Jewell never pays any attention to Mrs. Jewell's helpful and interesting additions to the conversation, but she often clarifies what her husband's rapid-fire style leaves obscure. Listening to them is schizo-stereo.

Fred Jewell has become a local character in Eastham, and he admits it. Cantankerous and contentious, he writes a lot of letters to the editor. But the Cape has taken him in—an outsider by birth—and he's now a member of the club.

"I criticized the library one day and they said, 'If you don't like it, why don't you do something about it?' So I got to work and painted signs and put them up all over town asking people to vote funds for an addition to the library. After we enlarged the building I started the historical society in a basement room. Then, when we bought the schoolhouse, everybody went to work painting, shingling, and repairing. We opened on July 4, 1966."

Mrs. Jewell said, "Fred's always into something. If it's not the school, it's something else. . . ."

"I got the plaques to put on the graves of the three *Mayflower* people who are buried in our cemetery. And now I'm putting snow fence along the beach just before Christmas to keep the sand from filling in the great marsh. There's plenty to do around here in the winter, but I hate to see the summer come."

Mrs. Jewell agreed. "You have to learn a new way of living here in the summer," she said. "Our grocery stores are so crowded with summer people, you have to know just when to go and when not to go. I always do my shopping on the high tide," she explained with a laugh. "Summer people are always at the beach when the tide's high."

"We were going to retire in Peking," Mr. Jewell said. "Then we thought about Honolulu. Now I think we'd rather be here. I like a place where you can see four distinct seasons."

The early spring sun was slanting through the living room windows, turning the camphorwood chests ruby and gold. As in many a Cape Cod house, a ship model was displayed. This one was a Chinese junk. It didn't seem out of place somehow. Only 150 years ago, they say, there were more men on Cape Cod who had been to Hong Kong than had made the overland trip to Boston.

RACE POINT

There is something about getting to the tip end of Cape Cod that is a little like standing in the bow of a ship as it cuts through the sea. We always went to Race Point because it was the bow—because we wanted to experience the special feeling of standing at the very extremity of this curious sandbar of ours. We would look out over the sea and say, "This is as far as you can go, kids. Over there is Europe—Portugal, maybe. Nothing in between but water." When they were young, this concept had little or no meaning to them, I'm sure. But we said it anyway.

Actually, if you drive as far as the road will take you on Cape Cod, you will not be looking eastward at Europe, but more nearly looking "back"—westward—at Plymouth. Because of its peculiarly clenched shape, the fist end of Cape Cod turns in toward the mainland, and the beach at Race Point, seemingly as far east as one can go, actually faces west —and the setting sun.

It was a theater for sunsets, a promontory especially dredged up from the ocean bottom from which to view the end of a summer's day. The great, fiery disc of the sun would slip beneath the rim of the sea, turning molton red, lighting the sky and the water and the sands first with ember-hot reflections, then with delicate pastel afterglow. Race Point was a place to stand on the edge of time, on the very rim of a world, where all the continental land was behind us and came slanting down, here, to the sea.

The beach is broad and curving at Race Point. It is a favorite place for striped-bass fishermen, endlessly casting into the surf; a place where gulls strut on the sands with a particular independence and where small, quick sandpipers sprint for food in the dusk.

We would park the car, kick off our shoes, and walk in sand still warm where our toes dug in. The kids would run ahead, silhouettes against the dying light. To them, a sunset was theatrical lighting, not a unit of measure.

On the sea's horizon a few sparks of white light would mark the presence of boats we couldn't see, and landward, in the dunes, lights also came on in the Race Point Coast Guard Station, a big white frame building, now painted pink by the sunset, soon to turn black against the evening sky.

"What do they do there, Dad?" Jenny would ask. "Do they have lifeboats? Do they rescue people from ship-wrecks?" I said I supposed they did, but I really didn't know. To a summer person, the Coast Guard Station was just a landmark that had always been—a sort of government-operated "outermost house," I thought, pretty good duty for whoever was there.

"Could we go up and see what's inside, Dad?" Chuck asked. I said I didn't think so. There was a front door, but it was always closed in July and August.

It was near Thanksgiving, a gray and blustery afternoon, when I parked my car in the deserted Race Point parking lot and found what seemed a path through the dry dune sand and rustling beach grass to the Coast Guard's front door. As I waited for an answer to my knock, I listened to the winter sea breaking on the beach—a stiff, aching sound, I thought, not warm and pliant as on summer nights.

The door opened, and a man in his forties, dressed in work blues, asked if he could help. I said I just wanted to come in and have a talk about the Coast Guard. Did they rescue people from shipwrecks here?

"Come on in!" said Bob Oliver with a friendly wave of his arm.

"Rescue people?" he exclaimed. "I'll say! Search and rescue is our primary purpose." Mr. Oliver, a Chief Bos'n's Mate, was in charge of the station. He showed me into an office—a desk and a couple of chairs, bare walls, and a well-scrubbed floor.

"Cup of coffee?" he asked. I said no thanks. I wanted to keep talking about those rescues.

"We've had 129 cases at this station in the last five months," Mr. Oliver said. "That's emergency calls. Get a lot more in the summer with all the pleasure craft. It's tricky waters around here, lots of places for summer people to get in trouble on shoals and like that."

I said I supposed the winter was a lot different. Mr. Oliver said it was.

"I was born and brought up here in Provincetown," he said. "It's not really a place where people like the duty, not in the winter. There's twenty men at this station and not one of them wouldn't take a transfer anytime from November to spring.

"The winds are northwest most of the time, and the sand really blows off that beach. Anything over 25 miles an hour, we have to move all our cars down to the airport for shelter. Takes the paint right off 'em, that blowing sand."

I thought he might be exaggerating. "You mean like a sandblaster?" I asked.

"Like a sandblaster. Turns the windshields milky white, too. Just like the old-timers used to do around here. They'd take a pane of window glass, then take a piece of cardboard and cut out the shape of a gull or something and paste it on the glass, then set it out here on this beach until the sand had blasted the glass everywhere except behind the cutout. Then they'd put it in a frame and sell it to summer people."

I'd never heard of it. Did this art form have a name?

"No name that I know of, but some of my boys are going to try it next time we get a blow here this winter." Mr. Oliver shook his head, just thinking of winter winds, I assumed. He went on talking without prompting.

"Winter rescue work is bad. It's usually fishing boats. They don't get lost like summer sailors do, but they have mechanical trouble or they lose a rudder or they get a net in the screw. Then we have to go out after 'em. Had one just the other night down off Wellfleet. Ten miles offshore and ten-foot seas." While Mr. Oliver talked, another coast-guardsman came in to listen. I guess visitors with tape recorders don't show up that often.

Since no Coast Guard boats are kept at Race Point, I asked where the rescue craft came from when they were needed.

"We have the forty-four-footer down at the wharf in Provincetown, but that's two and a half miles from here," Mr. Oliver explained. "Between the time we get a call for help and get out here around the corner, a lot can happen."

"Around the corner" means coming around the fist, several miles by sea, to the back of the hand.

"Fifty, sixty-mile northeasters are common here in the winter, you know," Mr. Oliver said, in case a summer person should be mistaken. "I remember one night there was a boat sinking right here around the corner—a dragger. We got the call. It was blowing about twenty-five to thirty then. We sent the forty-four out. By the time she got here, it was up to sixty mile an hour and seas was fifteen feet, it came up that quick."

I waited to find out what happened.

"Northeasters," muttered Mr. Oliver. "Terrible."

I asked about the fate of the dragger.

"Sank!" (Of course? I wondered) "But we got the men with a helicopter that came in from another station."

I asked about the cold. Fifteen-foot seas in midwinter sounded like more than a man could stand.

"Well, we've got heat on the forty-four. She cost $35,000. Nice boat. But it's cold anyway. Just damn cold, I don't care what people say about Cape Cod being warmer.

"Course, it isn't as cold as it was when I was a boy," Mr. Oliver said. "I can remember coming along this beach in the winter just after they built this station in 1935. I guess I was about ten. I'd come in here and go to sleep by the wood stove. It was colder then."

We got to talking about how the Coast Guard used to cover the Cape's great outer beach. "There used to be eleven stations," Mr. Oliver remembered. "Men from the stations used to walk the beach at night; they'd walk toward each other until they met at a halfway house, where they'd punch a clock and have a short talk and then head back. Winter and summer they did it. In the winter, when the sand would blow enough to cut the skin off your face, the man would get a cedar shingle and shape it into a paddle and hold it against his cheek for protection. We'd have to do the same thing today if we were still walking the beach."

The Coast Guard abandoned the beach stations long ago. Today, in the Provincetown area, they maintain the Race Point station, a fixed green light at Wood End at the entrance to Provincetown Harbor, a flashing red light at a place called Long Point, and a three-second white light, flashing once a minute, at Race Point, a mile and three quarters away from the station over a sand road.

"Charlie Powell's down there," Mr. Oliver announced. "Been there with his wife and two kids for four years now. He'll be retiring next month, though. Takes a certain kind of man for that kind of life—and a certain kind of woman, I guess. He comes out over the sand road twice a day, driving his kids to school and getting them home again every afternoon."

It was quiet in the station. In the next room a shortwave radio crackled with traffic every so often. I asked what the men did for recreation.

"Oh, we've got a pool table downstairs," Mr. Oliver said, "and three TVs. Play a little touch football out here in the parking lot after all the summer people are gone. The boys pick up a few town girls once in a while."

What about Thanksgiving and Christmas, I wanted to know.

"We have a tree here and a good dinner and all the fixin's. Ten of the boys get liberty and ten stay here. On New Year's we just switch. For the ones who stay behind, it's duty as usual—and you can just bet something will happen. It always does!

"Last year the *Jimmy Boy*, the biggest fishing boat in Provincetown, sank at the pier Christmas Eve. Right up over his pilot house in thirteen feet of water! Took two and a half days to get him pumped out and floating again."

Nice way to spend Christmas, I said. Mr. Oliver just laughed. "Bound to happen, I say. Winter's just a jinx."

We went for a look around the station. Upstairs is a dormitory, and above that a glass-enclosed lookout which is reached by climbing a ladder. When we got to the top, I looked out on the familiar beach. It was getting dark now; there had been no sunset. A curtain of black cloud rose from the western horizon and the wind buffeted the big plate-glass windows of the tower. Mr. Oliver looked up and down the line of the surf.

"You know," he said, "when a coastguardsman spends his first winter here, he looks out at that surf during a blow and he just doesn't believe it. Nobody's ever seen anything like it. The whole shape of the beach and the dunes can be changed by a storm. You can actually see the sand moving along in great rolling balls, moving, moving. . . ."

Radio equipment crackled and whistled. Voices came from somewhere and were routinely acknowledged. Colored lights on the equipment glowed.

I remembered that at the beginning of each summer when we had come back to a place like Race Point or Nauset Light, we saw a new landscape of sand, resculpted by winter.

"We can lose three feet of bluff in a winter northeaster," Mr. Oliver said. "One month last winter they lost twelve feet at Cape Cod Light. Summer people don't believe it when we tell them that."

We went down the ladder, then down the stairs. I had a lot of answers to the old summer questions now. Someday I would have to tell the kids what I had found out in November.

A BOOK SHOP
FOR ALL SEASONS

SUMMER reading. It was something I always promised to do at the Cape. Bring a good book, I would tell myself; there will be rainy days and foggy evenings. And bring books for the kids, too. Bedtime stories were as important while on vacation as they were back home in Connecticut. Quick Draw McGraw. Winnie the Pooh. The Roly-Poly Platypus. And after that, I might sit down with Beston or Thoreau and try to reinforce my feelings about the world.

One summer, when oldest Jenny was about fifteen, the reading bug hit her hard and she so often found a solitary reading place for herself in the dunes that we called her Lonesome Jen. For her, the time and the season and the place were right that year. For me, good intentions notwithstanding, it never quite happened that way.

Sometimes, when we were wandering through Province-town or Chatham or Wellfleet, a bookstore window would beckon with a display of "light fiction for summer," or "books about Cape Cod." The latter category always made me feel a little guilty, like an anti-intellectual slob who each year took pleasure from this Narrow Land but never found time to learn more about its history—social or natural. It was like enjoying clams, and knowing little else about them. Should I not know the names of those little birds on the beach or the difference between a herring gull and a black-back? What did I really know about the Pilgrims' landing on the Cape in 1620 beyond the fact that their "first en-counter" with the Indians occurred at First Encounter Beach in Eastham? Somehow, First Encounter Beach was not a place of history to me, but a parking lot choked with cars—a place to swim, fly kites, lie in the sun. Likewise the Cape itself: a place to explore, go to summer theaters, walk, eat, ride bikes, go shopping—anything but sit still. Maybe that is a typically American affliction, a compulsion to keep moving rather than contemplate. Whatever, the damning fact remained: despite the pangs of conscience, I read very few books in all those summers. The *New York Times*, yes; bookstores, no.

In Yarmouthport, one October day, when Route 6A was only lightly traveled, and autumn sun slanted warmly through golden and russet leaves, a man in a bookstore told me he didn't think there was such a thing as "summer reading."

"I don't see it," said Benjamin Muse, Jr. "Publishers make distinctions like that and they may have the market research to prove it, but I think a good book is a good book whether you read it in July or December."

Like a lot of other independent characters on the Cape, Mr. Muse is sometimes given to independent ideas. "I'm a loner," he says, "an anarchist." He looks to be about forty, a big, friendly man, the father of eight children.

The Parnassus Book Service, which Mr. Muse owns and operates, is one of the most singular operations of its kind anywhere. It is the biggest bookstore on Cape Cod, although Mr. Muse refuses to concede the local estimate that he stocks maybe 80,000 volumes, new and used. "That's playing with numbers," he says. "It's quality that counts, not quantity."

The store crowds the edge of the highway, a big, two-storied gray building with a high-peaked roof, a center door, and old-fashioned display windows on either side. Just to the right of the door as you enter is a jumbled rack of Cape Cod books. All the ones I should have read and many I'd never even heard of.

"The place was built around 1840," Mr. Muse explains. "It was a general store until about 1910. A religious sect occupied the second floor, where they had classrooms and services. The A&P came in for a short time, then it was a furniture store. I've been here about twelve years now."

Perhaps the most unique physical feature of the Parnassus establishment is a fresh-air bookstall that extends along the exterior wall of the building, eight feet high, twenty-five feet long, sheltered from the weather by a shedlike roof, but open to public browsing night and day, winter and summer. Several thousand second-hand books line its shelves. A sign welcomes all visitors, states that the price of each book (usually twenty-five or fifty cents) is marked inside the cover and to please pay inside. On Sundays, when the store is closed, customers are asked to drop payment through the mail slot in the front door.

"It's an honor system," says Mr. Muse, "and I think it works. If it doesn't, I don't want to know about it. That would spoil something."

He is a straight-talking character who, except for a certain soft accent, could easily pass for a Cape Codder born and raised. Actually, he was born in France, lived in South America, and went to school in Virginia (the accent) and New York.

"I first came to the Cape only fourteen years ago," he says. "I'd never been here before. Came up from New York one weekend in February to visit my mother-in-law in South Yarmouth. Before the weekend was over I had taken a lease on this store and bought a house. No rationale about it. In a flash, I just saw myself running a bookstore on the Cape instead of in Virginia where I had planned to move."

How had it worked out? Did the Cape's booming summer tourism mean a brisk and profitable trade in books to be read on the beach? Mr. Muse makes it clear he isn't just after the summer buck. He has a solid, year-round mail-order business, for one thing. He specializes in books about South America and the Soviet Union. He reprints rare works under his own Parnassus imprint. He deals in manuscripts and old letters.

"In the summer," he says, "we play host. We are entertaining people, really. They are our guests. We're open six days a week, usually until ten or eleven o'clock at night. I never close the doors as long as there is a customer in the store. That means 1 A.M. sometimes. The way I see it, these people are down here to enjoy themselves for a day or a week and I like to welcome them."

And what about the winter?

"In the winter we work harder. We catch up on our mail, buy books, attend to mail orders. I wouldn't say I like the winter better, but in the summer we're really prisoners here on Cape Cod—prisoners of our own success."

One or two customers were browsing through the friendly clutter of the store as we talked. Stacks of books, mostly used, reached from floor to ceiling. Boxes of new books just received from publishers lined the aisles. The place had the warmth of an old-fashioned general store. Mr. Muse leaned against the open drawer of a file cabinet and did a little bookkeeping while he remembered the pleasure and the pain of summer.

"We used to be able to go to any beach we wanted," he said. "Now we can't. If you want to drive from here to

Hyannis, it takes two hours in summer, but fifteen minutes in winter. People ask me what's a nice restaurant around here in summer and I have to tell them I don't know. We never go anywhere in July and August.

"They've overpromoted and overadvertised the Cape. We don't need all this Chamber of Commerce-type hoopla. I tell this same thing to the local newspaperman when he comes around to try and sell me an advertisement. You don't have to advertise as long as you have a product. If it's good, people will come to you.

"I'm not trying to bring more people to this store. I couldn't take care of any more. If I had more people, I'd have to pave that area in front of the bookstall and make it a parking lot and paint white lines on it and put up a sign saying 'Don't drive beyond this line.' Then I'd have to increase my staff and move my own office upstairs—and suddenly I've lost the whole character of my operation."

Mr. Muse just shook his head as he went back to filling a mail order. "The Cape has already sown the seeds of its own destruction. I don't know what's going to happen."

He came here first on a weekend in February. If he had come on a weekend in August, he might be running a bookstore in Virginia today.

"I'd rather see some other kind of natural disaster hit the Cape," says Mr. Muse. "Summer makes strangers of us all. A good heavy snowstorm draws people together."

THOSE WERE THE DAYS

SUMMER people didn't get much involved in the pro and con battles that preceded the establishment of the Cape Cod National Park and Seashore. Oh, we heard something about it after John Kennedy became president, and we knew that Cape Codders were divided on the question, but it wasn't until the summer of 1964, I think, that the arrival of the feds had any tangible effect on our summer customs one way or the other.

"Who's the guy in the green uniform?" one of the kids asked almost incredulously as we drove toward the usual entrance to Coast Guard Beach in Eastham. There he stood, wearing a Smoky the Bear hat, smiling pleasantly at everybody and demanding a one dollar admission and parking fee. The whole scene came as a jolt. *Pay?* To go to the beach? What was happening in our summer hideaway? What bureaucratic forces had descended upon us—in uniform yet —to regulate one of nature's most unregulated joys?

At Eastham, only the oceanside beaches were affected by the new regimentation. The bayside beaches—with their still magically nostalgic names—remained under the jurisdiction of the towns and free of federal control. Since our cottage was located inland, equidistant from the Cape's inner and outer shorelines, a typical summer day often consisted of going down to the sea twice—once to the bay and once to the ocean, the choice sometimes depending on the tide and sometimes on a curious selection system regulated by the children. This required going at least once to every beach in town, never going to the same beach twice in succession, and so on.

The older ones would test the younger: a brother or sister was considered a true initiate when he or she could name all the beaches and in proper order. I can still hear the voices in the back seat of the car:

"Pauline B. Hatch, First Encounter, Kingsbury, Cook's Brook, Thumpertown, Sunken Meadow, Coast Guard, Nauset Light . . ."

Of course, there are really only two Cape Cod beaches— the great outer strand and the sheltered bayside. The various given names serve only to identify certain arbitrary sectors of sand, meaningless if you walk the length of the beach, useful only if you are looking for approach roads.

As our years passed, it was unmistakable that the Cape beaches and their adjacent parking lots were becoming ever more choked with people and cars. I considered myself wily enough always to find a place to park or a section of beach sufficiently open for a game of Frisbee. But by the early sixties it was getting tough. Further, the pleasures of the beach aside, there seemed to be a lack of things to do, ways for would-be explorers to probe the Cape's hinterlands. Somewhere in Truro, you were told, was the spring from which the Pilgrims first took fresh water. But how to find it? Somewhere in Wellfleet were the remains of Marconi's original trans-Atlantic wireless station. But where? For the summer person who sought more than gift shops and straw-hat theater, the Cape needed a good guide service.

In part, the National Park Service has become just that. True enough, they charge a dollar a day to park at the beach, and apparently some diehards still regard the federal presence an intrusion only slightly less odious than the Redcoats, but the men and women in green uniforms have done many good works already, such as facilitating the summer people's search for Pilgrim Spring and the Marconi ruins.

One September day last year, after the tide of summer visitors had ebbed, I was driving more or less aimlessly around some of my old haunts on the Cape, when I spotted one of the new National Park buildings on high ground in the wild dune country "back" of Provincetown. I had never seen the building before, but I remembered the place. Earlier, a crude wooden platform had stood there, raised above the sand on poles, from which a tourist could gain a view of the area. (Chuck had once tested my binoculars there; the eyepieces were too far apart for him, I remember.) Now a modern, low-roofed, octagonal structure with many glass walls squatted amid the scrub pines. Dune grass, growing in rows like a hair transplant, betrayed the newness of the landscaping. A sign said that this was the Province Lands Visitors' Center. I walked in.

Inside, the Visitors' Center consists of a large, airy, circular room with a spiral staircase in the middle leading to an upper level. A fine view of the ocean and the nearby dunes is seen through the large window walls. There is a book stand, a display of marine specimens and artifacts, and a counter, behind which stood a lean, weathered-looking man. His uniform was crisp and his manner was friendly. He was Warren Perry, ranger-in-charge. After talking with him for a short time I realized I had come upon a fount of information about Cape Cod. Would that my kids could have heard him explain things in those summers long ago!

"Yes, sir," he said almost respectfully, "things'll change now that September's here. We get a different crowd once summer's over. Older folks, most of 'em. Shopping for a retirement home, maybe. They're not looking for gift-shop junk."

The Visitors' Center looks so much like a summer facility that I asked when it would close for the winter.

"Don't ever close, sir," said Perry. "Not here. Just Mondays and Tuesdays, but we're open the other five days. Course I'm alone most of the time on winter days. Bring my lunch. But just the same there's always enough visitors to keep it from getting lonely. Look here," he said, pulling a clipboard out from under the counter. "We had over a thousand people in here last December and over a thousand in January, too. Not bad for dead of winter, is it? It actually starts picking up in February and March."

What, I asked, was the count for a summer month?

Warren Perry talks with the irrepressible enthusiasm of Hubert Humphrey. Even ordinary facts sound important when he discloses them.

"We had 77,163 visitors last August," he said with gosh-durn pride.

Warren Perry was born in Provincetown forty-seven years ago. His wife is a school teacher. During World War II he served in the Coast Guard for four years in Europe. He started with the National Park Service in 1961. Now he wears the uniform of the federal "outsiders," but he's as salty an individual as Washington could have found for his job.

"Go downtown in summer?" he says. "Never happen!" Like many Cape Codders, Perry holds down two jobs in the summer.

"I start driving a beach taxi for Matt Costa the first week in July. Drive for him all summer on my days off." A beach taxi is a four-wheel-drive vehicle with oversize tires which takes tourists on long rides through the dunes and along the beaches of Provincetown. Warren Perry has been doing it for a long time.

"I used to drive regular passenger cars before we had the four-wheel-drive cars," he says. "I used to do it in a 1936 Ford with the air let out of the tires. Arthur Costa still has the old pictures of us. Used to call Arthur the 'King of the Dunes.' There were only three rigs for hire in Provincetown in those days. One of 'em was run by the undertaker, Porcky Noones.Now there are twenty-two or twenty-three. I make four to six trips a day with people. I drive slower than some of the drivers because I have more to say to 'em." Perry laughs at himself a little when he says this, but by now I was sure it was the truth. Wind Warren Perry up and you get the darndest folklore spiel since Barnum introduced pygmies.

"There may not be much work around here in winter," Perry says, "but it's really not so bad. If you want some fish for supper you go down to the pier and ask one of the captains for a flounder or two. We're the only fishing port in this country where it's a tradition to give away fish. Ask the captain, Can I pay you? and he'll wave his arm and say, 'Get outa here' and laugh. I go down for fish maybe three times a week in the winter. Course, there's some smart alecks who'll take a couple of fish from one captain and hide 'em in their car, then try to get a couple more from another boat. That's what we call chiseling. If the fish is for your supper, all right. . . ."

A few visitors walked around the Center while we talked. They went up the spiral stairs to get a better view from the top, browsed through the books and pamphlets for sale. Perry sold two copies of Thoreau.

"Wintertime, there's room to talk," he went on. "Some of us will sit around and try to remember things. What was down there by the cold storage? someone will ask and I'll say it was Lou Pitney's place when he sold Blue Bird tonic. And there was Frank Rowe's nice big house on the hill and Mrs. Phipps' place with the beautiful fruit orchard, peaches and plums, all gone now. Remember R. L. Shute? Coal, five bags for 95 cents."

Perry leaned back against the wall, looked out the big window toward the sea. His leathery brown face makes his eyes seem white and sharp. Even at forty-seven, he seemed to be looking way back. Provincetown has changed so swiftly that even a young man can see the change.

"Everybody's after the dirty American buck," Perry said. "We'll never get the town back. It makes me bitter. If the old-timers could come back to life, I don't know what they'd think. There was one nice old place with a beautiful lawn and beautiful Cape Cod garden with zinnias. What happened? They filled the lawn with concrete slabs then let a caricature artist work there. Took out the Cape Cod windows, put in store windows. Take that place across from the Methodist church. . . ."

I didn't know where he meant, but it didn't matter.

"They painted it an *off-pink!* I say let's get the town back to what we had before. But I doubt we can. I doubt it."

Winter is a pause in Provincetown's headlong rush to destruction. Some people have called it an outlaw town. A rum-runner town. A homosexual's haven. A place for the quaint strugglers of the twenties and thirties who were called, innocently enough, "the starving artists."

"Now it's something else," says Perry. "It's a welfare town in winter. Used to be, young people would come down here and work summers, then go home. Now they stay, on welfare. There's so much shoplifting at the A&P it's making plainclothes moonlighting jobs for some of our policemen.

"There's still jobs to do in winter; nobody needs to steal. You can make a buck if you hustle. There's boats to be caulked sometimes or a stuffing box to be fixed. When I was younger, we'd paint a whole boat bottom for $15 in the winter. Even now there's some winter jobs in the pool hall and bowling alley. Some people collect pine cones for the Christmas market. Send them to the city florists.

"Bayberry business is poor. The price for bayberries is very low now because of the artificial scents that've taken over. Don't smell like bayberry candles when they burn, but they're cheap."

In the distance, while we talked, I could see a fishing boat slowly making its way southward toward Nauset.

"That's the *Nancy and Debbie*," said Perry matter-of-factly. I didn't see how he could tell. The boat looked like a spot of black and white with toothpicks.

"Sometimes you can *find* money in the winter," he went on, still looking at the boat. "Lately people have been picking up old bottles in the dump behind Cliff Nelson's riding stable. They sell 'em to a place called the "Bottle Door" in Dennis. Friend of mine took eight bottles up there last week and made $32 off 'em. I guess they sell 'em for quite a price to the summer people.

"Then sometimes we can get along without money at all.
Let's say somebody wants to renovate a room in his house.
You give him a hand. Then maybe he builds a fireplace for
you in return. No money changes hands. Neither one would
have any, most likely anyway, but one scratches the other.
When the Moors restaurant burned a few years ago, every
carpenter in town was there to help rebuild it."

The Moors. I had eaten there so many times in summers
past. Good Portuguese soup. Great fish. But I never knew
it had burned down.

The Visitors' Center looked like a place that would take
a lashing from winter winds in any direction. I asked Perry
how he stood the weather.

"Gulf Stream's changing things," he said. "The winters
just aren't as cold or snowy as they used to be." Once again
he went to look at a chart. "See here. The coldest day last
October was 33 degrees. The coldest day in November was
30. And in December, 23. Course, we had some snow, but
it's really the wind that does the damage. A northeast storm
chews the Cape away like a bulldozer, moves the sand all the
way from Nauset Light down here to Race Point. Makes
new bars and spits as it goes. Changes everything.

"Worst storm we ever had, though, was the hurricane of
1938. That's when Eugene O'Neill's house was taken right
off the beach and out to sea. He was a famous playwright.
Used to have an apartment down at John Francis' place at
557 Commercial Street. They put on his plays at a wharf in
the East End called the Triple Sevens.

"Storms do all sorts of mischief around here. Just this year the hull of the ship *Frances* showed up on the outer beach. She was a wooden ship that went down forty, fifty years ago, I think. There it was for a few days in full sight, then the sea took it back. Gone now."

I knew it was getting near closing time. I didn't want to use up Warren Perry's whole afternoon with talk. I said I'd come down again next month.

"You can hunt pheasants and quail down here in October," Perry reminded me, "and ducks in November. There was people here in the old days who made winter money by hunting black ducks for market. All around Pilgrim Lake they'd come in. If you got a good lot you put 'em on the night train to Boston to sell. I had an old Marshwood shotgun with a Damascus barrel. Paid three dollars for it. I'd wait for a storm to drive the red-leggers in over the dike or into the marshes by Wood End." Perry gave me a big, genuine smile.

"Winter's not so bad here, you know. Come on back later this year and find out for yourself!"

Quite a guy, I thought. Green uniform and all. And I wished again he'd been around sooner. The kids would have mimicked his Cape Cod accent, but they would have learned something from him.

KURT VONNEGUT, JR.

HAVING been at times employed as a magazine editor and having harbored an ambition to write for more years than I cared to count, I often wondered about the Cape as a place where one might settle down to the typewriter and do some good work. It was hardly an idea that I could put to the test as a summer person, of course. I never even brought a typewriter along with all that paraphernalia from Connecticut, nor did I have the time to write so much as a salty limerick in all those summers. Or was that just my excuse?

I knew people who lived on the Cape and made their living as writers—and I knew would-be writers who lived on the Cape and made their living doing something else. Perhaps the Cape's mystical qualities had nothing to do with the matter. Perhaps the salt air, restful landscapes, muted colors, and general serenity of the Narrow Land were really no more conducive to writing than a one-room, ground-floor apartment in noisy Manhattan.

Yet the idea had a homey, hideaway quality—a Cape Cod cottage, a view of the bay, a driftwood fire, walks on the winter beach—wouldn't that be an environment in which a man might at least find the best that was in him? Hadn't such a life inspired Thoreau and O'Neill and all the others who had passed this way at some time in their writing careers?

One day in New York, long after I'd given up any vague notion of making Cape Cod a permanent address, I talked with a man who had lived on the Cape for many years, making his living as a writer, winter and summer, until he became one of America's foremost novelists—and then he left the Cape, apparently for good.

I pressed Kurt Vonnegut, Jr., for his impressions and insights until I think he became annoyed with me. I knew what summer was like; I wanted him to tell me that winter was different. I expected he might say, Yes indeed, winter is a time for a writer to really get something *done* on Cape Cod. Alas for preformed opinions, I should know that they invariably wither in the face of facts.

"You're trying to get an answer that isn't there," Mr. Vonnegut said impatiently. "You have to take into account that there are some lives that don't change radically with the seasons, and on the Cape this would be the lives of people in places like Cotuit and Barnstable.

"I lived there twenty years, right near the Barnstable courthouse," Mr. Vonnegut went on. "I was a free-lance writer and I could live anywhere I wanted to. I had a large house with a lot of kids in it—three of my own and three adopted—and Cape Cod was a padded cell where children couldn't possibly hurt themselves when they were growing up. It worked out very well. I'm glad I picked the Cape.

"It was only after my kids grew up that I began to feel that I was in the middle of desolation—simply not enough company. It's hard to be integrated if you're in a business as specialized as mine. You don't have associates. You go to parties, and people are vaguely mystified as to what you do and embarrassed if they haven't kept up with you. The social groups on the Cape are composed of people in typical kinds of businesses—restaurants, construction, that sort of thing. They all talk shop. Everybody talks shop. That's what holds a social group together.

"In New York there are people for *me* to talk shop with. On the Cape, I had to talk about building or zoning or the new high school."

Kurt Vonnegut is the author of the successful novel, *Slaughterhouse Five*. A best seller. His novels—*Player Piano, The Sirens of Titan, Mother Night, Cat's Cradle, God Bless You, Mr. Rosewater*—are enormously popular with young people. He is a celebrity. Perhaps he outgrew Cape Cod. But he lived there long enough to know the place well.

We went back to the winter business. "You can get the statistics on the weather somewhere, I'm sure," he said a little wearily. "Actually, there's no difference between summer and winter. Barnstable isn't invaded by tourists in summer. There are no big tourist traps, no large hotel, only one small bar. I knew the people who came down in the summertime because they always come down in summertime. The families have had summer houses there for generations.

"The climate is like Maryland. The first winter I lived there, winter never came. That happens some years. The snows, when they come, are quite romantic, real Christmas-card snows. They come suddenly and soon disappear. It isn't the weather that's bad on the Cape. There just isn't enough interesting company to take you *through* the winter."

His first summer, like mine, was 1951.

"I lived on Commercial Street in Provincetown, right at the beginning, opposite the Texaco station. The house was on the bayside beach. I wrote most of *Player Piano* there. It was beautiful, that summer. I liked it. But I didn't want to live in Provincetown year round because the reputation of the schools was very poor."

Otherwise, Mr. Vonnegut, what did you think of P'town?

"It has always been, from its beginnings, an outlaw town. Yankees all over the Cape have been suspicious of those foreigners in Provincetown. Especially those who couldn't speak English. Later, in Prohibition days, it was an important bootlegging port. Then, of course, there have always been artists in Provincetown, and Yankees conventionally regard artists as lunatics and sexually loose."

No writer spends every hour at the typewriter. What did Mr. Vonnegut do for recreation on the Cape after he settled in as a permanent resident?

"Oh, everybody goes to the town meetings. I'd do that.

And I was president of the amateur theatrical society for a while. My wife and I did a lot of acting. A couple of times I took jobs for a short period, but I was writing all the time too. I taught in a private school in Sandwich for a semester. When the trains were still running, I took a job for six months as a copywriter in Boston.

"Another time, I got a franchise and started selling cars. I was one of the first Saab dealers in the country. It was a financial disaster, but interesting."

I asked if he would go back. Did Kurt Vonnegut, born and brought up in Indiana, miss Cape Cod?

"I have no permanent affection for the place. The people who are genuinely in love with it are Yankees who have been there for several generations. Other people *say* they've fallen in love with the Cape, usually soon after moving there. They are generally retired people writing home to friends in Cleveland telling them how happy they are on the Cape. I question this. I think it's a very boring place to be."

THE SHELLFISH
WARDEN

ALMOST everyone who goes to the Cape in the summer pictures himself harvesting all the shellfish he can eat, particularly clams. Every year, as we left Connecticut, we would promise ourselves that this was the summer we'd find a great digging spot and bring home our legal limit (one ten-quart pail) every week. After all, the delicious little devils were there for the taking, were they not? Must be millions of them, if you can only find the right place.

Somehow, we never did. It was, I learned, a disappointment shared by many summer people. There just aren't enough clams to go around any more, and by August, which was usually our month at Eastham, the flats were cleaned out. Failures notwithstanding, we always tried. The ritual began with a trip to the town hall for a license on our first Monday morning. A lady behind the counter would nod her appreciation of the fact that the Barnards were back again this summer. "Now where's your cottage again?" she'd ask, and we'd say that it was the Voorhis place on Meetinghouse Road, and she'd say, "Oh, yes," as if she remembered from last year. Then she'd fill out the license and hand it over the counter along with a steel ring two inches in diameter.

"That's how big a clam has to be for us to keep him," I'd explain to Chuck. "Two inches long." He would take the ring and hold it in his little fist. "I'll measure 'em, Dad," he'd say, and out we'd go in search of our chowder makings.

There were two places you could go—to Salt Pond, a beautiful, round little kettle hole hard by Route 6 near the center of town, where clamming is allowed every Sunday, or along the great bay itself, near a beach called Pauline B. Hatch. We usually went there, walking far out across the sandy flats at low tide, a small scouting party on a vast wasteland, armed with a pail, a clam rake, and the optimism of gold seekers, our eyes scanning for the telltale little holes that said *maybe* a clam lurked neck-deep below. Then we would dig, turning up black sand and mud from beneath the tawny, sea-washed surface, pawing through the slurry with bare hands and, with luck, finding a few of the elusive creatures, but never many.

One day, Chuck and I were returning to the parking lot with a few clams in the bottom of our bucket, when a spare man with a sun-browned face stepped up and said in a friendly way, "I'm afraid that's a violation."

We looked into our pail, quite sure that every one of the

clams, few though they were, was longer than two inches.

"Not the clams," the man said, "the shovel."

Then we knew. Chuck was carrying his small sand shovel, not to dig clams—which is definitely forbidden—but because at that age he always kept it with him when we went to the beach.

"I'll just give you a warning this time," the shellfish constable said, "but remember, son, shovels and clams don't mix."

Many summers went by, and Chuck had grown taller than his father before I saw that constable again and learned who he was. His name is Phil Schwind—Captain Phil Schwind, some people call him, though he's not a captain of anything—and although Eastham is his home, he is known up and down the Cape as a shellfish expert, part-time author of folklore, and a generally salty character. A few summer people may get to know him, but winter is a better time to have a talk.

"I work seventy hours a week in the summer," he said. "No time for anything." We were sitting comfortably in the living room of his small, snug house on Samoset Road. It was a Sunday in November. Hardly any traffic moved on the road to the beach.

"For thirty years I was a fish pirate and now I'm the local fuzz. It's ridiculous! Of course, the worse the pirate, the better law-enforcement officer you make." Schwind laughs at his own joke. "But we don't have bad enforcement problems. Just usually summer people who don't know any better."

I told him about the shovel.

"Don't matter to me who you are. I've given violation notices to a selectman, a state cop, an FBI man, and a member of the House of Representatives."

Schwind appears to be in his fifties, a nonstop, interesting talker. He holds a long *aaahhh* sound between sentences so you can't interrupt him; his wife says it came from being a radio operator. He writes a column called "It's An Ill Wind" for the weekly paper, *Cape Codder*, he lectures twice a week in summer at the National Seashore centers, and he is the author of several booklets full of shellfish facts and folkloric nonsense.

I asked him what the winter was like for a shellfish warden.

"Well, I don't work seven days a week, but there's still plenty to do. There's as many people digging clams at the Salt Pond on a Sunday in November as there are in July. You might not believe it, but it's true. If you like clams, you don't just like 'em in the summer, do you?"

I said I loved clams but could never find enough of them.

"It's a fact," Schwind nodded. "We don't have enough. We've got 7000 people a year digging for clams, and the town is only four miles long. We're overfished, especially in the summer."

If Schwind, and wardens like him in other Cape towns, did not transplant clams by the hundreds of bushels into town waters there would be none at all. With license money, he buys clams from commercial dredgers, then plants them where people dig.

"I start in April, usually. Put 440 bushels into Salt Pond last year. Went clear around the shoreline one and a half times. For every three bushels you put in, folks dig out four. The difference is how much they grow between seeding and harvesting.

"Put 100 bushels into Nauset Marsh. And 60 bushels of sea clams along the west shore. Sometimes it seems people are digging them up as fast as I can put them in. Those little clams must think they're on a kind of crazy elevator until they get to two-inch size—they're up and down, up and down all summer."

Wouldn't it be easier, I asked, if he just passed out buckets of clams to the people with licenses instead of everybody working so hard to hide them and then find them.

"Nobody'd want their clams *that* way," Schwind answered, slightly incensed at the thought. "You have to dig your own clams or they're no good."

He was a fisherman before he was a warden. "Came down here in 1934. I'd bought this land when I was seventeen. Worked my way through Boston University at the Quincy waterworks. Then I tied in with an old fisherman. He furnished the know-how and I furnished the bull strength and awkwardness. We did everything. Handlining. Net fishing. Dragging.

"There's no reason I shouldn't be a commercial shellfisherman even now, but I guess it wouldn't look right for the warden. But I'll go eeling this winter in the Salt Pond."

We talked on through the afternoon. How he's trying to propagate oysters by a Japanese method; how scallops live their two-year lives; how mussels can destroy a clam flat; how razor clams can dig themselves down a foot or more into the sand. And the predators and how they kill: moonsnails, horseshoe crabs, starfish. He showed me some of the slides he uses in lectures.

"I've got three or four thousand pictures," he said proudly.

I asked if he had a copy of his best-known book, *Clam Shack Clammer.*

"Ayuh. It'll cost you a dollar, though."

I paid.

"Never mind how this house looks," he said as I was leaving. "Built it all myself. Brought second-hand lumber down here on the roof of my car in the thirties. Only had a hammer and a saw and didn't know a thing about carpentering. That's why she sags here and there."

Phil Schwind. If I'd known him years ago, Chuck and I might have found that great spot where all the clams were hiding.

"They're not clams, you know," he corrected me. "They're quahogs. Altogether different creature." How many times did I have to be told? On Cape Cod, a clam is a quahog—*Mercenaria mercenaria,* to be exact. Of course, just to be confusing, there are also shellfish on the Cape that are called clams—*Mya Arenaria,* used for steamers. Would I remember all that? Probably not, but a summer person could learn a lot on a Sunday in November.

CIRO'S PLACE

IT was a long weekend in February, Lincoln's Birthday, and a wet, cold storm was lashing the New England coastline from Connecticut north. The weather notwithstanding, a friend and I headed up Interstate 95 for the Cape. Reservations? Nonsense. Who would be going to Provincetown at this time of year and in this weather? We discovered a surprising answer: in the 1970s, a lot of people may go to the Cape on any weekend of the year. As winter's early darkness fell that day, every motel and rooming house still open between Truro and the Provincetown Inn had hung out its no-vacancy sign. Other frustrated travelers, buffeted by wind and rain, unwilling to believe that there wasn't a room to be rented, trudged in and out of any place that showed a light. But Provincetown was sold out. It looked like a long, late ride back up the Cape.

It's one thing, we thought, to be miserable, but quite

another to be both miserable and hungry. So we decided to eat. With the storm tossing the old elms that border Commercial Street, and rain turning the narrow road into a rushing canal, we headed for an oasis of warmth and Italian food. Fortunately for stranded tourists that night, Ciro & Sal's, one of Provincetown's most popular restaurants, was experimenting with staying open on winter weekends. As we burst through the door, sodden and tired, we could see that the off-season experiment was working: the place was jammed.

In summer, Ciro's is a booming, reservations-only, stand-in-line type of place. Families come early, are seated in one of two main dining rooms, waiters in jeans and sandals rush about, and as many as 500 people may be served between 5 and 10 P.M. Ciro's atmospheric, candle-lit, brick-floored dining room is really the cellar of an old house. On winter evenings, a roaring fireplace fire sends cheer and woodsmoke throughout the place; rich smells of cheese, garlic, wine, and oregano spice the air; and a pleasant collegian named Debbie Jennings Minsky greets and seats the guests.

"You haven't found a room?" she said, her eyes widening, when we told her our story. "Can't believe it! Well, sit down and have dinner and we'll see what we can do for you."

It couldn't happen in summer, but on this wild February night, a room was found. Like passengers on a storm-tossed ship, we shared a special companionship with the people around us.

"John Ciluzzi's going to open up one of his heated cottages for you," Debbie said, coming back to our table. She had been on the telephone. "He eats here all the time. He's glad to do it. Friend of Ciro's."

Ciro Cozzi is about fifty. In Provincetown, he is a man with many friends. He was born in New York City, went through World War II, came home to study at the Art Students' League under the G.I. Bill and ended up, a "starving artist," in Provincetown. He has a round face, a happy smile, a head of bushy, curly hair, a light easy voice, rather like the actor Peter Falk. In a turtleneck sweater, he looks more like an artist than a restaurateur. Provincetown is his home year round.

"I like it best in the winter, though," he says. "In the summer I'm so busy I can seldom get out into the dining room and talk with people." Ciro is a friendly person, and on the long, drear weekends of the off-season, he makes his restaurant a friendly place.

"There's no plan to our menu in winter," Ciro says with a reckless smile. "We just rotate a few of the most popular dishes, something different every week. Some Saturday nights in winter we serve two hundred dinners. The people aren't the same crowd who come in the summer. Very few kids. No stolen ashtrays. They come because they love the food and enjoy a leisurely meal. Some come from as far away as Boston."

In summer, there is no shortage of eating places in Provincetown: seafood-and-lobster types, Portuguese, French,

Yankee, and Italian. How did one of the many become so famous and successful? How did it all begin, Ciro? We were sitting at a small table near the fire. Candlelight shot ruby flashes through a glass of Campari.

"I bought this house for $8700 in 1947. It sounded like $870,000 at the time. An uncle helped me raise the $1400 downpayment." The house faces Commercial Street, the town's main stem. It is a large, Yankee-built Victorian structure with many rooms—and the capacious cellar.

"I met my former partner, Sal, in 1951. He was a Korean War veteran. We got the idea to open up an after-hours sandwich shop during the summer months. Sal had $120 and I had the cellar. We were both Italian, we came from families who enjoyed good food, but we didn't know anything about cooking. Nothing. I could cook eggs for breakfast, maybe, that was all. But we gave it a try. I was a waiter in another restaurant at the time. I'd get off work about 9 or 10 P.M. and come back here and start making sandwiches. Sal made 'em too.

"I don't know whether it was because we served better sandwiches or because we had the prettiest waitresses, but business really took off. We had some atmosphere, the girls were all in bare feet and short shorts, but most important of all, we stayed open late. We'd serve until 2 A.M.; couldn't keep the people out of here.

"But the neighbors were up in arms. They couldn't get any sleep, so they were going to take us to court. One of the town selectmen, Bill White, gave us a chance; he said if we'd close by 11:30 every night, we could keep operating. Well, that was the end of the sandwich business. Now we had to become a restaurant. But neither of us could cook. . . ."

The big logs in the fireplace were beginning to burn hot now. Arriving guests held their hands, palms out, to the warmth. Ciro looked into the fire, remembering the years.

"Okay. No more sandwiches. We had to turn to basics. Spaghetti. Spaghetti and meatballs, spaghetti and sausage. After a few weeks we got up our courage to try a chicken dish. I bought a nice big bird at the market, but nobody told me it was a fowl and needed a little parboiling. I made a *cacciatore bianco* with it, and when the first customer ordered the dish, Sal and I watched him through the kitchen door to see how he liked it.

"Well, the poor man started to sweat profusely. And he chewed and he chewed and he chewed. When he got up to leave, I asked him about the chicken.

" 'The flavor was excellent,' he said. Then he admitted it might have been a little tough. After that I had a talk with my mother about chicken."

In the postwar years, Provincetown was just a summer place. Each year Ciro and Sal closed their restaurant the day after Labor Day and went back to work as house painters. "One winter," Ciro remembers, "I also drove a truck between New Haven and New York to make ends meet."

Sal left the partnership after seven years. He now runs a restaurant of his own at the other end of town. But the two former sandwich makers have remained fast friends.

Does a New York boy miss the big city?

"I go back now and then," Ciro says. "It's exciting. But I'm a country boy now. I've got Cape Cod sand in my shoes. I don't like the city any more. I'm doing what I like best— a little painting and drawing in my free time, and the restaurant."

The first time I ever went to Ciro's was as a summer person, years ago. The food was marvelous, and the cellar was cool. Somehow, though, on a night when a nor'easter rattles the glass and the fire hisses the dampness out of the wood, the food tastes even better.

THE FLEET

MACMILLAN WHARF, at the center of Provincetown, juts hundreds of feet into the harbor. It is straight, cement-paved, and crossed at the end like a T. In summer it is a strolling place for tourists—a place where you can take a ride on a sailing ship, go out on a charter fishing boat, take scuba-diving lessons, or watch coastguardsmen do chores on a small cutter stationed dockside. Perhaps the greatest attractions for summer people are the boats of Provincetown's small commercial fishing fleet, which are usually tied up at the top of the T. *Jimmy Boy, Nancy & Debby, Liberty.* Sturdy, honest-looking little boats, all well kept, painted green and white and black with orange masts, their decks stained but scrubbed, their colorful nylon nets hung out for repairs. Sometimes you can see a crewman working on one of them, but for the most part the boats just rock quietly against the pier and answer no questions about what they do or where they have been.

Sometimes, I remember, we were at the end of the wharf when a boat came in loaded with fish, and we would watch them unload the tons of slithering, silver cargo and see it move into the Seafood Packers Company warehouse.

"What kind of fish are those, Dad?" one of the kids would ask, and I wouldn't know. Haddock? Halibut? Cod? A land-lubber is always lost in a fishmarket. Even if the fish were big, it was a guessing game. One day we looked inside the rear of the warehouse and watched a gang of strong men in rubber boots as they drove big hooks into the luminous flanks of some giant fish. Pulling on the hooks, it took two men to slide one of these big stiff creatures along the floor and up to the rear of a truck. Becky's hand crept into mine as we looked into the great blind eyes of these dead levia-thans. I asked one of the men what they were. Blood dripped off the shining hook in his gloved hand.

"Horse," he answered, too busy to say more. That meant Horse mackerel, or tuna to kids who loved tunafish sand-wiches.

In summer, gulls perch on the roof of the packing house in tight formation, like white and gray fighter planes with folded wings parked on a carrier's broad deck. Looking back toward the town from the end of the wharf, you see the Provincetown "skyline," a long low fringe of small houses, mostly white, looking like a toy village at the edge of a blue sea. Looming over all is the granite shaft of the Pilgrim Monument—a 252-foot Italian renaissance-style tower which seems strangely out of place in a Portuguese fishing port.

In November, MacMillan Wharf is a gray slab of concrete surrounded by slate-colored water. The tourists and the charter boats are gone. Only the real fishermen are left.

There are about forty boats in the fleet now, and you seldom see them all together at any one time. A few were tied up side by side one day after Thanksgiving when I was retracing the steps of summers past. Park Ranger Warren Perry had told me I should talk with Frankie Reis if I wanted to know what it was like for the fishermen in wintertime. I found Frankie inside a small cubicle of an office at the end of the pier. A former fisherman himself, he is now the man who sells all the fish for a cooperative of about thirty skippers. Seven days a week he is on the telephone to New York, Boston, New Bedford—anyplace there is a market for fish.

A shortwave radio receiver whistled and whined on Frankie Reis' desk. Occasionally, the voice of a fishing-boat captain could be heard, garbled talk to the uninitiated ear. Reis knew what they were saying. They were telling him they were coming in, what they had for a catch, how much weight, how long it would take.

"Winter fishing is five times harder," he said to me between telephone calls. "But a fisherman can make more money in the winter because the prices are higher. In the summer, you have every Tom, Dick, and Harry fishing—out of New Bedford, out of Boston, out of Gloucester. They catch so many fish in the summer that prices go to peanuts. We can be going along getting fifteen, sixteen cents a pound for whiting in the summer when all of a sudden Gloucester comes in loaded with whiting. Then New Jersey the same.

When that happens, a Provincetown skipper can't give his fish away."

The office is a clutter of marine hardware, files, charts on the walls. It has one door and one window. A fisherman came in to pick up a check. He wore a heavy wool shirt, red and black plaid, and black rubber boots on which fish scales reflected light like animal eyes at night.

"Fishing's the only real industry this town's got," Frankie said after the man leaves with his money. "They tell about the tourist business. Well let me tell you: seventy-five percent of the income from tourists goes to people who leave town after the summer is over. Shopkeepers, motel keepers, restaurant people. They take all the good weather and they take all the loot. The fisherman makes his money here and he spends it here."

A dark-faced, stocky man, middle aged, came in from the pier. Joe Corea. "Talk to him about fishing in the winter," Frankie says. "He did enough of it to know."

The man looked out the glass-paned door toward the sea. "Anybody coming in?" he asked Frankie.

"I've got the big fellow coming in Sunday with 75,000."

Seventy-five thousand pounds of fish. A trip. A boatload.

I asked Joe Corea how long he had fished out of Provincetown.

"Thirty-six years," he said, still looking out the door.

"Which one is your boat?" I asked.

"The *Papa Joe*," he said. Pause. "The same boat for thirty-six years. I don't have it any more. Haven't been fishing for three years now. Gave it up. The winters was too much."

Frankie Reis was on the phone again. Joking, cursing. The radio crackled. The small room smelled of wet clothes and old boots and rope. It was a quiet day. A lot of the skippers were making a four-day weekend of Thanksgiving.

"I've done all kinds of fishing," Joe Corea said. "Seining. Tuna fishing. Scalloping. Swordfishing. Shrimp fishing. I've done 'em all. I was a skipper in St. Augustine, Florida, when I was fifteen. But I came home to Provincetown. Too hot in the summer down there. Too cold in the winter up here.

"It's a different kind of fishing in the winter. Mostly codfish and yellowtails. When you can get a day good enough to go out, you get paid for it. But January and February to the middle of March, it's rough. You're lucky to get thirty-six hours of good weather. You drop the fish on deck and they freeze solid. How you going to clean frozen fish? So you gotta keep pouring water on 'em.

"You can't stay out as long in the winter. In the summer, we used to be out three or four days, maybe five. I've stayed out as long as eighteen days. In the winter you have to watch that barometer.

"The future of this business depends on how far we have to go for fish. What's killing us now is the foreign boats—Spain, Russia, Italy. The Russians came first in 1950. They don't leave us too much, and they don't throw anything away. Not a scrap. Their factory ship processes everything right there. I've seen sixty or sixty-five of their boats in one place. It looks like a city when you see them all together.

"But you know, those Russians aren't so tough. Or maybe they're not so dumb. They don't fish here in the winter, they quit about the end of December. Too cold for 'em."

Frankie was listening. He laughed at the Russians. "Bastards," he said.

The future of commercial fishing may be uncertain for the fleets skippers, but summer and winter they're the true elite of the town.

Frankie explained while Joe Corea smiled with approval. "Summertime around here, most people have to have two, three, four jobs to make it. In the winter, the line at unemployment is twenty miles long. That's where you meet everybody once a week. But you almost never see a fisherman there. He can be 'unemployed' of course, but in another way. All he has to do is lose his net and he's out of business for a while. But he doesn't collect unemployment. He's lucky if he collects insurance."

The captain and the businessman compared some figures. They agreed that the average net—those pretty nylon things that summer tourists photograph—costs $1500 to $2000.

"When you put that net over the side of your boat," Capt. Corea said, "it don't belong to you any more. Hook it up on a wreck or a snag and you've lost a net. Insurance? Yeah, we got insurance. But that costs about $6000 a year for every boat in the harbor, plus $400 a year on each man in the crew."

In fishing, as in everything else, the price of independence comes high.

As I walked back down the pier toward town, I remembered all those warm summer days when the fishing boats were ornaments of the season. It took a cold, gray day in November to show me they were also the year-round bread and butter for a hardy bunch of men.

A CRANBERRY FARMER

CRANBERRIES. What did I know about them all those years? I knew, first, that they grew on the Cape, and second, that they grew in places called bogs. Sometimes, in summer, we would be driving along a back road and would come upon a sort of sunken meadow covered with scrubby growth and crisscrossed with drainage ditches. Somehow these places always looked abandoned. The kids would say, "Is that a cranberry bog, Daddy?" and I would say "Yes," but dubiously.

"I don't see any cranberries," Jenny might say, and I would answer, "Well, they're small berries," or something like that. Small and red and tart and delicious, I knew. At Christmastime and Thanksgiving they were simmered with sugar until their skins popped, then cooled in a mold and brought to the table with the turkey, a small ruby-colored mountain as traditional as the bird itself.

But first, cranberries had to come from Cape Cod, from farmers. I had never spotted a farmer in his fields or seen a cranberry bog cultivated or sprayed or harvested. The little red berries were to me, as they are to most of the Cape's summer visitors, a mystery crop, something that happened when we weren't there.

"The bogs turn reddish like this after the harvest," Mr. Arthur Handy explained. It was November in North Falmouth. We stood by a roadside barn, looking inland over cranberry bogs that stretched below us like rectangles of velvet carpet in the dusk. As manicured as a tea plantation, they seemed, glowing with the color of clouded wine. The berries were gone now, harvested a month or more ago. The color we saw was in the small leaves of the cranberry vines themselves—hardy, ground-hugging little plants which have grown and prospered in Cape Cod soil as long as settlers there can remember.

Arthur Handy is in his fifties, a gentle-spoken man with the soft accent of the Cape. In Massachusetts, fifty growers probably account for 75 percent of the crop, and Mr. Handy is one of these. He owns 140 acres of bogs. His father was a cranberry farmer and his grandfather too. He'd like one of his sons to become the fourth generation in the business, but he doesn't know if this will happen.

"If they want it," he says, then adds, "but it isn't an easy life."

We walked with him along the edge of the velvet. A small

ditch separated the bog from the surrounding green banks. The bog itself was bisected here and there by small irrigation canals.

Why don't summer people ever see any activity around the bogs? I wanted to know.

"Summer's our quietest time," Mr. Handy said. "We might be putting a little liquid fertilizer on or irrigating or weeding, but the real work starts with the harvest, beginning about September 20 and lasting up to November."

He rolled open the door to the big old barn with an echoing rumble. Inside, hundreds of empty boxes were stacked high, and a big piece of farm machinery stood by one wall. A few ripe, red berries were scattered about on the board floor. It was still and cold in the barn.

"There are our harvest boxes—three boxes make a barrel, a barrel is a hundred pounds. We get about ten dollars for a barrel from the cooperative. Some years it seems as if it costs us almost that much to raise them." There was a dignity about Mr. Handy: the sort of man who could take a loss without whining, or make a profit without boasting.

"There's no doubt we have an overproduction problem that's hurting prices. Massachusetts raises two million barrels a year, but we only sell about one and a half million." He sighed mildly. "The rest has to be thrown away. It's a shame. Shame to waste anything that's good."

After the harvest, the farmers clean the bogs by flooding them with water. Dead leaves, twigs, and other debris float to the surface and are skimmed off. Then the water may be left on the bog to protect the plants from the deep cold of winter.

"We never run out of things to do," Mr. Handy said. We had driven to two more of the Handy bogs at another location in North Falmouth. The bogs, all rose and russet in the gathering dusk, looked like romantic landscape paintings.

"I think this is rather a lovely spot," Mr. Handy said quietly, understating his feelings, I thought, for fear a stranger might not understand a man's love for his land.

"There are eighty acres here, eleven of them in cranberries. My father bought this in 1929 or '30. But it's an old bog. Probably planted in the 1860s or 1870s." One perennial crop for over a century. Never replanted. Never neglected.

"We're busy in the winter too," he said. "Every third year we sand these bogs, spread a hundred cubic yards or more per acre. Takes a day to do an acre. Sometimes, if we get six or eight inches of ice on a flooded bog, the boys will get the sand trucks going full speed on the ice and cut the wheels—and away we go!" Mr. Handy smiled at the memory of the winter sport.

"We spread the sand right on the ice in winter. Have to keep at it, sanding. Without it, the vines grow rank and the yield goes down."

Cranberry vines grow in sand, then, I discovered, not in bog peat. There may be a foot of sand on top of the peat, with cranberry roots growing into it four inches or more. "Sand is what keeps the vines short," Mr. Handy said again. It was something a summer person might never guess.

"Course, frost is another problem. We can have frost as late as June, and as early as August." He ticked off the risks of the business calmly. "We used to flood the bogs if a frost was coming in spring, but now we spray them with water instead. It doesn't drown the plants so much."

He stooped to pull up a piece of vine and hold it in his strong hands. "There are the buds for next year," he said, peeling back leaves from the stem. "The blossoms are already in there. Now if we should get a real stinger of a frost next spring, we might not get a crop off these vines for two years.

"Cranberries," said Mr. Handy, "are somewhat of a gamble. If you guess wrong . . ."

I asked him if tourists ever visited the bogs. "Sometimes," he said, slowly. "I don't discourage them. Our problem is with the small boys. They like to jump the ditches and chase after frogs and turtles. They're not so much interested in the cranberries."

We went for a cup of coffee and held our cold hands around the mugs. "It's too bad more people don't know about cranberries," Mr. Handy said reflectively. "They belong on the Cape. Course they're grown other places too. Wisconsin and New Jersey, mostly. But they began here. The oldest bog is in Dennis, they say. Dates back to the 1700s. Man's name was Howe. He was an old seaman, I think. He cultivated the first wild cranberries. They were just growing around the dunes with the sand blowing over them."

Some of the vines are still called Howes. Some are called Early Blacks.

"We've been experimenting with some crosses. One is called a Franklin. It's nice looking and a little larger, but it's not that wonderful a berry."

Why, I asked, does he keep trying to increase the yield in the face of overproduction.

"Well, we have to look to the future," Mr. Handy said. "Wouldn't want Wisconsin to get ahead of us."

It was almost dark when we said goodbye. I watched his truck head back down the road toward Falmouth. A noble sort of man, I thought. I was a little ashamed that I hadn't known more about his business before. Somehow, if we loved the Cape, we should have found out more about cranberries. Now, in November, I had.

SUMMER STRANGER,
WINTER FRIEND

WE had done business with each other in Eastham summer after summer, for how long? A dozen Augusts, certainly. His store is called the Superette—a tidy little food market in the center of town. One might call it a plain place, I suppose, yet for us it was somehow touched with summer's magic. It was the place we went each day to buy groceries and light-bulbs and postcards and charcoal and bug spray and, above all, candy.

"Three pieces, Dad?" Chuck would plead. Of course, three pieces, just don't eat them before breakfast. The picture is still so clear: little people in bare feet and bathing suits standing in front of the candy counter, picking, choosing, grabbing, deciding, putting back and, finally, coming up to the man by the cash register with their collection for the day.

"That'll be twenty-five cents," he'd say sternly, but with his eyes smiling, and one of the small hands would offer coins and then snatch up the loot.

"Hey, want a bag?" But they were usually gone by then. I'd put down a few items to be added up, and the man would always have something pleasant to say.

"Going to be breezy." Or perhaps, "High tide's at noon today." We knew each other, no mistake, if not by name, certainly by every other sign of recognition. We were about the same age, I think. We watched each other grow older, summer by summer. Then, one summer, I didn't come to the Cape any more.

Two or three years passed before I saw the man again. It was November and I was driving through Eastham one late afternoon. I saw the sign—"Superette"—and I heard summer's voices again. Three pieces, Dad?

There were no cars in the parking lot but mine and, in the store, no customers. I went in just to remember, to see if it was all the same, all as I had left it. He was standing there behind the counter, just as he always did.

"I remember your face," he said right away.

"I used to come here a lot in the summer."

"Oh, sure, I remember your face all right."

"I remember yours too. I didn't know you'd be open."

"Open year round. Always have been. People I bought this store from stayed open all year, so I do too."

"When was that?"

"Oh, twenty years ago."

"I came first in 1956. You were here then."

"Yes, I was here in '56. . . . I remember you."

"My name is Charles Barnard."

"Glad to meet you. I'm Ed Brown."

Fifteen years may seem a long time finding out a man's name, but in summer on the Cape, nobody seems to have a name. Faces may become familiar, but there's little time for introductions.

"You won't have any trouble writing about the Cape in the winter," he said. "Just write down, 'It's very good,' and then close your book. That's all you need to say."

I asked him if he meant business was good.

"Business is terrible!" he said. "It doesn't pay to stay open in the winter, not in January, February, or March anyway. But at least there's time to talk to someone."

One or two people came in to buy a few groceries on their way home. I looked for the candy counter. It was still in the same place. M & Ms, Good & Plenty, Necco's.

"Summer business must make up for the winter," I said.

"You can sell anything you put in the store in the summer. Summer people will buy anything at any price."

I remembered all the ten-cent kites we had bought here. Some had gone out a thousand feet or more, tough little wind climbers made of thin paper and flimsy sticks.

"Kites? Can't keep 'em in stock. I'll start the summer with seventy-five boxes, twenty-four kites to the box, but they won't last. Did you say ten cents? No more. They all want the plastic ones now. Dollar."

I asked him if he was a Cape Codder. He didn't sound like one.

"I was a summer person myself once," he said. "My family came here every year from Winchester, Mass., when I was a boy. 1919 was my first summer. Then, later, we decided to stay.

"I've seen a lot of other beautiful places in this world that I never want to see again. Guadalcanal. Bougainville. New Guinea. Now I'm where I want to be. I like it here. I like to remember this place the way it was back when my kids were little. I guess that's why I like the winter."

I knew what he meant.

REALTORS

It is in no way unusual, I'm sure, for summer people to look about the Cape and dream of buying some land or a quaint old summer house. We "looked" from 1957 on, always putting off the day when we would get really serious about buying anything. What was the hurry? The land would always be there, wouldn't it? And there seemed to be no end to the years ahead—or to the acres of scrub pine or the network of back roads with hardly a house for miles.

Nevertheless, the occasional real estate signs always beckoned. A place of our own to come to. Not just in August, but anytime—spring, Thanksgiving. Hmm. And then maybe rent it out just enough to pay the overhead. It's a classic bourgeois dream, and it has sold cabins in the woods across America for half a century and made many a real estate broker happy. On Cape Cod in the 1970s, most brokers couldn't be happier. They're not just renting cottages on the beach any more—they're dealing in expensive, scarce real estate, and they have waiting lists. The procrastinators of the fifties have been replaced by smart-money buyers who realize that Cape Cod real estate is one of the best investments around.

"Don't put your money in the bank!" says John Sherwin, an independent-minded broker who operates in the Wellfleet-Truro area. "Real estate is going up ten to fifteen percent a year around here—and land, well, name your price. I handled a piece of land not long ago for a client who paid pretty good money for it and then turned around and put it right back on the market again for double what he paid. He sold it within a year."

The National Park certainly made Cape land more scarce, and more year-round visitors has made it even more in demand. The Cape in winter is no longer a beach community that boards up its windows after Labor Day.

"Better than one third of our summer renters come back to become buyers," says Sherwin, "and they often want to buy the place they're renting, especially if they've taken the same house for several years."

Of the more than five hundred houses which Sherwin has available for rent each summer, only about twenty-five are also available in winter. "Eventually," he says, "ninety percent of the houses here will be year round."

What does it all cost? "In summer," says ex-Air Force officer Sherwin, "you might get a two-bedroom place for $750 a month—and you can easily pay up to $2500 a month for bigger places."

And in the winter? "Hundred a month. Hundred and
fifty, maybe. And for that you get a house that probably
rents for ten times that figure in the summer. You're also
getting some of the Cape's most beautiful months between
September and June."

But had I not always wanted to *own* a piece of the Cape,
a little high ground somewhere with a view of . . . what? The
bay? Where summer's waters for my young waders had so
often been "as warm as a bath?" The ocean? Where I would
always remember Polar Bear Jenny plunging into the big
waves she and I called "swimmers?"

"Land with what we call a 'distant water view' is selling
for $17,000 a half acre now," John Sherwin said with a
broker's smile. "Right on the water the same half acre could
bring $40,000. Everybody wants waterfront until they hear
the prices, then they think of settling for something else. I
can get you a half acre of wooded land for $8,000. No view
though."

I don't think I could live in a fresh-built Cape Cod house.
They always look as if they'd just come green from the
sawmill, all raw wood and new shingles, waiting for the sea
air and the fogs, the sun and salt and wind and sand to
mellow them into some gentle compatibility with their sur-
roundings. All the same, there aren't enough old houses to
go around, so the Cape is dotted with clusters of bright new
homes, many of them looking more like suburbia than the
Pilgrim's Narrow Land. And just as expensive as suburbia,
too.

"If you'll take a house in the woods," says Sherwin,

"they're selling in the middle thirties. Houses on the beach, $60,000 to $90,000 for the average place, nothing exceptional. If you're looking for rock-bottom, a cabin, say, no heat, no land, no view, just a place to make coffee and change your bathing suit, you might find something for $14,000."

John Sherwin says he has 2000 people on a waiting list for houses. "Fifteen hundred of them would buy something tomorrow, if we could find the right place for them."

If this sounds like work, work, work (and plenty of commissions), Sherwin doesn't seem like a man who is in total pursuit of the almighty dollar.

"Not after Labor Day at any rate," he says. "If it's low tide and I want some oysters on a winter afternoon, I just put my little cardboard clock on the door and say 'Back at three o'clock' and I take off. The bluefish and the bass run right up through the end of October, and the fishing is great in the fall. You can get thirty, forty fish in a couple of hours, then you give them away to whoever will take them. Sometimes, on a fall afternoon, you just leave the fish you don't want on the dock for anyone to pick up."

Barbara Lovely, a gracious and intelligent lady, is a real-estate broker in Orleans. She recognizes that what's good for her business isn't necessarily good for Cape Cod.

"Man is loving the Cape to death," she says. "The Cape Cod Chamber of Commerce has a policy of getting as many bodies onto the Cape as possible. But this drive for the tourist dollar has often brought the wrong kind of people."

We talked about the winter. Were summer people invariably happy with the Cape after they became permanent residents?

"I have a cardinal rule for people who think they want to come here to live year round. Come in September some year and rent a place from September to June. See if the Cape is for you.

"I've known some older people who pulled up their roots elsewhere and came here and were disappointed. We don't always have the things they want. Concerts. Plays. Library services. We need a lot more of these things.

"And for the young people, there isn't enough to do out here in winter. We have drug and booze problems like everywhere else. Everybody who moves to the Cape doesn't end up happy. There are just as many family problems here as anywhere. Too many people come here thinking they will leave their problems behind, somehow. Then they find that they only brought them along. Cape Cod is no cure-all, summer or winter."

Straight talk. It made me think. I had a fantasy once, long ago, a mini-drama in which my life and family fell apart, shattered. Then I saw myself on the Cape, alone by a familiar cottage, knowing that soon everyone would return, that we would all be together again, that the magic of the place would do it, would draw us like a breeze in a sail and heal us with sea-air balm. The first part of the dream eventually became a reality, but now I knew the second never would. It would take more than a house on Cape Cod to do that. A real-estate broker had just told me why.

OYSTERS IN THE SNOW

THE salt ice on the beach was like large, silvery fish scales,
thin discs almost the size of saucers, stacked in windrows,
marking the farthest advance of the last high tide, mingling
there with whiter snow and a thick mulch of pulverized
marsh grass. Over all was the hissing sound of new snow
propelled by a gentle wind, swirling onto Chequesset Neck
in Wellfleet. It was December. The winter sun was setting
behind the dark snow clouds, casting its last light across the
water. I'd never been on a Cape Cod beach in a snowstorm
before.

Out in the tidal flats I could see my friend in his waders,
silhouetted black against the flaming water, stooping now
and then to search for the oysters, then dropping them into
a basket. He made no scratch or splash that I could hear; the
only sounds were the snow and the crunch of my feet in the
frozen grass and sand. It was cold, far below freezing, I

remember, and I walked up and down the beach to stir my circulation, wishing all the while that I had brought some high rubber boots for oystering.

A pretty place, I thought, using the phrase we had used in summer whenever our explorations discovered some quiet spot where we might watch a sunset. There had been, first, The Pretty Place. And later, The New Pretty Place. I think it was Becky who named them that way. Did she know I was here now? That I had discovered a Winter Pretty Place? I would have to tell her about it. Hey, Beck, you should have seen it, not at all soft like our summer evenings, but diamond pure, flashing cold, the water as black as in an old inkwell.

I turned my back to the wind, kicked through debris on the beach, so much of it colored plastic offal without the decency to decay: Clorox, Breck, Blue Bonnet. When I looked up again, I saw that my oystering friend's figure was no longer stooped, but standing straight. He was coming in.

Kirk Wilkinson and I worked together for the same company in the same building in Manhattan for many years. He was an art director and I was an editor. We knew each other slightly, enough to know that we both went to the Cape in the summer. Sometimes, in the elevator, we would compare notes on what was new in Wellfleet or Eastham. He owned his own property, I knew, had built tennis courts, and went back to Wellfleet in the off-season. I envied him those pleasures.

Now Kirk is retired on Cape Cod, a strong and energetic

man who has left behind the world of magazine publishing, bought an art gallery in Wellfleet, winterized his summer house, and settled down to the life that so many of the Cape's summer people dream about for themselves.

We sat by the fire in his living room. The oysters were in the kitchen now, waiting to be opened before dinner. Outside, the snow was still falling.

"We bought this land in 1951," Kirk said, his eyes seeming to look back across the years. "We moved into the house in the summer of '52. We started coming up at odd times almost from the beginning. We made a family tradition of being here for Thanksgiving, for instance. It was a lonesome place in the early years. After Labor Day you could shoot a cannon down Main Street in Wellfleet and not hit anything. Now, in October and November, you can see lights in houses all through these woods. There are always enough people to get a good game of tennis going on Thanksgiving."

What is it like, I wanted to know, to come here to stay? To settle down in a house which was once a vacation place, to hear the winds of winter in summer's pines?

"I was euphoric in my first winter," Kirk answered. "I'd wake up every morning and say, 'Damn. I can just decide anything I want to do today.' I'd had enough of New York. Thirty-three years of it. Lunch at the Century or the Algonquin. The same faces . . .

"In those days, I remember that when somebody left New York, when they disappeared to do what we've done here, you sort of wrote them off because you felt New York was the center of the world. But when you're on the Cape, looking back at Manhattan, you realize this is nonsense."

The second winter was a little different. The retired man was still his own boss, but "It seems long, by February," Kirk says now. "Spring comes late on the Cape, and you get a little stir-crazy waiting for it."

Like many other residents who can afford it, Kirk and Caps Wilkinson travel off-Cape when the winter's doldrums seem longest.

"My hairdresser is in Paris right now," says Caps. "And our oyster man is in Nassau."

"We've discovered beautiful old Boston for one thing," Kirk adds. "And we walk. Five miles a day isn't unusual in winter for us. You can do that much in Wellfleet without ever crossing a blacktop road. The traces of the Old King's Highway can still be found in the woodlands. And old houses and schools. We take a map and a compass and a pedometer sometimes, and we're learning more about Cape Cod than we knew in twenty years as summer people."

What about the pleasures of the beach, I asked. It must be wonderful to have the shore to yourself, especially in the fall.

"Funny thing," Kirk said. "Now that we live here, I didn't go swimming all last year."

HOMETOWN PAPER

THERE are several newspapers on Cape Cod, but they are all weeklies save one, so the average two-week summer person is usually not exposed to much local journalism. Vacationers from the Boston area tend to keep on reading the *Globe* every morning, and New Yorkers stick with the *Times.* A tabloid-size paper called the *Cape Codder* is published in Orleans and distributed all over the Cape. In Eastham, I remember, we would sometimes buy a copy of the *Provincetown Advocate,* not so much for news but for local color. The paper had a quaint, small-town quality and one of the most picturesque logotypes in the business: a panoramic steel engraving of the Provincetown waterfront, circa 1870.

Occasionally, one would meet a dedicated vacationer who said he subscribed to the *Advocate* year round. "Keeps me in touch with the Cape over the winter," was the usual reason given. I often wondered what there was to keep in touch with. Until recent years, Provincetown was a winter ghost town with every activity but fishing shut down tight. Nevertheless, the *Advocate* was over one hundred years old. A lot of American newspapers had gone out of business in that time. It had to be doing something right, summer and winter, to survive.

"I wouldn't be living in Provincetown today if it weren't for the *Advocate.*" The man who said this looked a little out of place in the small, cluttered office of the fishermen's cooperative. His accent wasn't that of a local boat captain, and his clothes, although casual, seemed to have been selected with some care. He was in his forties, a tall, good-looking, well-spoken man. His name, he said, was Gayle Charles. "But I'm sorry I can't tell you anything about the winter here because this is my first year. I haven't seen a winter yet."

Gayle Charles is secretary of the Fishermen's Co-op. In a brief time at that job he has become an effective spokesman and negotiator for fishermen's interests, not only in Massachusetts but at the federal level as well. But he is not a native Cape Codder; he is a worldly man who has come to Provincetown with his family to live, perhaps for the rest of his days.

"I first came to the Cape as a child in 1930. We were from Maplewood, New Jersey. Just summer people who came here for vacations. I always liked the place. Even came back and lived here a short while after college. Then I left the States and didn't return for twenty years."

But before he left, Gayle Charles, almost fatefully, decided he would keep track of what was going on on the Cape by subscribing to the *Advocate*. The subscription followed him to many places through the years.

"First I spent two years sailing around the world in a yacht," Charles says. "The *Advocate* was forwarded wherever there was mail. I read that paper even in New Guinea and the Solomon Islands. I always got it. And I would read about Provincetown and remember my summers here."

Charles settled down next in South Africa. He was in the rock-lobster business briefly in Cape Town, then he went into advertising. He met an English girl from Portuguese West Africa, and they were married. After ten years in Africa he moved to London, where he became managing director of an advertising agency.

"And after four and a half years of selling cigarettes and automobiles, I'd had enough," he says. "One day I was reading the *Advocate* in London when I saw a help-wanted ad for this job as secretary at the co-op. I applied by mail and got the post. So, after twenty years, I came back. Cape Town to Provincetown. It's very strange—like fate."

Gayle Charles says he and his family are going to stay in Provincetown now. "I'll never go back to advertising. I'm content to be here. We're going to do a lot of sailing and walking, and we may go shopping once a month in Hyannis. And, oh yes," adds Charles with a smile, "I'm going to keep on reading the local paper."

I've been reading it myself ever since I took my off-season pilgrimage to the Cape. That's not unusual; the paper says that more than half its subscribers live off the Cape these days, many of them in New York City. Like the community it represents, the *Advocate* has changed since those earlier years when we bought it to find out what was playing at the movies.

"It's owned by a bunch of New Yorkers now," the locals will tell you, "bunch of pot-smoking hippies."

Maybe that's what I like about it. The paper is young and brash and seems beholden to no one. It jumps into local squabbles, it has a sense of humor to go with its sense of involvement, a sense of mischief to go with its sense of profession. Its century-old logotype is unchanged, like an outdated Currier & Ives print across the top of the front page, but the news is livelier, and its several regular by-line features are as genuinely Cape Cod as chowder. If you can't be on the Lower Cape in January but would like to be, reading the columns in the *Advocate* can be the next best thing. Samples:

From "My Pamet," by Town Father:

A feller'd have to be some sort of a clod not to extol the beauties of this January day. Granted, the temperature never did get above the mid-thirties, but the sun was so bright and the sky so clear that you could forget that thin red line of the thermometer. And the thin layer of cirrus cloud had the friendly, lazy look you see when the membrane closes over the eye of a dozing cat.

From "Orleans Scenes" by S. Stewart Brooks:

As I write, the sun is just setting at the end of what has been a lovely, sunny winter day. The last of the birds are leaving the feeders to seek shelter for the night. Down on the still-frozen Cove where narrow stretches of open water border the shore, a blue heron spreads its broad wings and flies off into the gathering dusk. Out on the ice innumerable Canada geese and black ducks huddle down against the cold.

From "Alongshore" by John Bell:

Ice-making cold and high winds frequently lined Mac-Millan pier with idle fishing boats sporting waterline whiskers of salt ice. Last Saturday, no Co-op boats were out. The gang keeping warm in the office went out briefly to box Capt. Alfred Joseph's bags of sea scallops before they froze in the open air. The wind rushing through the open doorways of the pier shelter felt colder than the breeze outdoors.

Town Father again:

We took a bit of time to do some outdoor chores today —split up some hard pine boards for kindling, and laid axe to some scrub pine in the round, and the frost-permeated wood split like ripe melons. . . . then we built a fire on the hearth and now the smell of hot resin fills the house most pleasantly.

Brooks:

Despite the recent bitter cold, the ice in the Cove hasn't been thick enough for men to safely venture out on it, chop holes and spear for eels, except on one or two days. On one of those, in the late afternoon, I watched two men on the ice as they finished their eeling for the day. The sun was already far down the western sky and dusk was coming on when they brought up the last of the catch from the bottom. But I could see it had been a successful outing, for as each headed shoreward, I noticed that the large container on their sleds was just about full, for it took strong pulling to get it moving over the ice.

Town Father:

The wind is out of the east, a real limb tosser, and the barometer is low on the quadrant and still falling and there's a steady, drumming rain beating against the south wall of our venerable old Cape Codder. We've turned on almost as many lights as we require in the evening and still there seem to be dark, gloomy corners in the rooms—and the smell of the side chambers permeates the house—a mixture of dried pine boards and mellow fruit and wool clothing.

The *Provincetown Advocate* comes out of a small brick-front, cinder block building near the center of town on

Commercial Street. E. J. Kahn III is something I always wanted to be—a twenty-four-year-old newspaper editor. It is his first year in the job. His chestnut hair is shoulder length, his work shirt comfortably faded, his blue jeans mellow from washing. His back-room office reflects the *Advocate's* genteel poverty—bare walls, a single, unshaded flourescent light, a telephone, a typewriter, a ragged bulletin board, and a desk made by stretching a door across two old typewriter stands.

"I came to the Cape for the first time when I was a year old," says Editor Kahn. "Twenty-three years ago. We have a house in Truro . . . my father's house. That's where I live now." His father is E. J. Kahn, Jr., the writer and, perhaps not incidentally, one of the four owners of the paper. The other three are Malcolm Hobbs, publisher of the *Cape Codder;* a Sunday editor of the *New York Times;* and a New York advertising man.

"They've called us a *New York Times* training school for radical lefties," says Kahn. "We've made a lot of enemies already: the people who think we're radical—which we are —or Communist, which we're not."

It is a Thursday morning, the day before the paper comes out. Kahn has been up late the night before, putting a sixteen-page edition to bed. Aside from the columns, the paper is a two-man operation; Kahn and an even younger associate, John Short, write the whole thing.

"I think we've turned the paper around financially," Kahn says, opening a stack of mail on his door-desk and patiently dropping the press releases, one by one, into a big wastebasket. "By this December we should be showing a profit. We're shooting for a 10,000 circulation this summer."

They may make it in today's Provincetown. A thousand new voters have been added to the registration rolls in the last two years—about a third of the electorate. The newcomers are, for the most part, young seekers. E. J. Kahn's *Advocate* speaks a cleaned-up version of their language. They are an important part of his audience.

"When I was a kid," says Kahn, "we never came to P'town from Truro. I remember seeing some movies in P'town, but my parents always gave me the impression this was a place to stay away from. I'm sure that's why I'm here now. No question. I just came to the conclusion somewhere around college that my parents were all wrong about what was good for me and if they said this place was bad for me, then there must be something good here—and there has been. A really hard experience. There's not much bullshit in Provincetown in the winter. It's too tight a community."

What does a young, Harvard-educated journalist see as his future on Cape Cod? There's a note of despair in Kahn's answer.

"I think the Cape is about to lose everything. It's in its twilight. Look, in one week in Truro two developers have submitted subdivision plans that will produce ninety-four new homes—that's 200 new voters in a town that has only 700 right now. That's a power block that could control the future of the town. These people are coming in with no sense of what the town was or what needs to be protected. When it comes to development, I'm a little reactionary." Kahn sweeps his long hair off his forehead.

"All my friends are trying to talk me into going to Nova Scotia. They say that's where the Cape is now—the way the Cape *was*, that is. Land is cheap up there, you can own your own home—which you can't do here. They say that's the next place to find what we were looking for here."

And give up such a promising start on a career?

"You can always start your own paper. . . ."

THE OUTERMOST HOUSE

I HAD heard about the Outermost House long before I read
the book—a small cottage in the dunes where Henry Beston
had lived alone for a year in the 1920s. I knew where it was
in Eastham, about a mile out on a long peninsula of sand,
with the ocean on one side and Nauset Marsh on the other.
There are now a few other cottages on the narrow strip, but
when Beston wrote, his was the only dwelling south of
Nauset Light. And it was as far east, as outermost, as you
could be on the Cape. Therefore its name. I had always
known where it was, but as long as I hadn't read the book,
I felt no particular urge to go see the house.

When we were all in Eastham, we used to talk about
taking a walk out there, and I once knew some people who
wanted to possess the place by renting it for a month in
summer. Later, after I had read Beston and appreciated
him, it seemed too late. Beston was gone, my summers had

139

died, and with them a lot of things that might have been.

"That book is still one of the most popular we have to sell," Park Ranger Warren Perry told me one day, much later, when I was browsing around his bookstand at the Visitors' Center in Provincetown. "Some folks come in here and they ask me, sorta embarrassed, they say, 'Wasn't there a famous book written about a Cape Cod outhouse?' " Warren thinks that's funny. It happens a dozen times a summer, he says.

"I've never been out there," I said.

"It's not far," Warren said. "You know the way, don't you?"

I said I did. As we were talking, it was afternoon on a windy but not too cold day in February. The anemometer on top of the Visitors' Center was registering fifty-mile gusts, and I knew the sea would be pounding Beston's winter beach much as he had described it long ago. Suddenly, I decided this was the day to go to the house.

Mine was the only car in the big Coast Guard Beach parking lot when I got there—it had always been full on summer days. The wind pulled at the car door when I opened it, and the sound of the sea behind the dunes was louder than the noise of the wind. This was as far as I would drive. Although there is a trace of a road through the sand to Outermost House, a sign warns against trying it with less than four-wheel drive. From here, then, I would walk. I turned the collar of my fleece-lined coat up high, stuffed my hands deep into the pockets and moved out along the ruts of the sand road.

Above, pieces of low-flying cloud swept in from the sea like shreds of old sails carried away from some ship by the storm. It was slow walking, as it should be, I thought. Beston wouldn't want a blacktop road leading out to his house or any signs pointing the way. There are none, only the rolling ruts carved through tougher turf, with the dunes rising like a sheltering barrier on my left. The sea is just there, behind them, I said to myself. I could feel and hear its presence, like a great breathing, the aspirations of a laboring giant. I didn't want to look at it just yet; I would stay low and inside, following the road along the marsh to my right. It was the most direct route and sheltered, too.

Within ten minutes, I came upon the first house on the peninsula, a little white cottage built on pilings driven into the sand, its windows shuttered tight against winter. Two or three other houses appeared farther on, one of them a large modern thing with great expanses of glass. It wasn't there when Beston lived on this beach, I was sure.

When the surf crashes on the Great Beach, each wave breaks into pieces of all sizes. Some of the falling pieces are the size of bedsheets, writhing as they topple, but staying intact to the last instant of destruction. Other chunks break off in the wave's headlong rush toward the land—pieces as big as a lace curtain or as small as a doily. All are eventually shattered and flattened and rolled smooth by the hard ramp of sand which they climb. But all these pieces of wave propel tiny droplets into the air, minute particles which are then freed from the power of the sea and given over to the power of the wind. Do sailors call this spume? Or sea fog? It is salty on the lips and sticks to eyeglasses, I know. I could feel it settling on me as I walked, and I could hear the source of it growing louder now as the sandspit narrowed.

I could see only about fifty yards through the salty fog. The marsh was a flat tableland, its surface inscribed with canals, and the water seemed to be rising. Within a few minutes I could see that low portions of the road ahead were now acting as channels. Long fingers of pewter-colored water were marching toward me, each rut in the road becoming an irrigation ditch. Soon the whole road was filling with seawater, and I was forced to choose a route through higher ground in the dunes to my left. It was slower going here, and still no sign of the house. The sound of the surf was stronger. With each crash I thought I must be able to feel the vibration shivering through this narrow sandbar.

The house had been moved once or twice, I was told, moved back from the eroding beach into the higher dunes. It was hard to imagine one place being considered more secure than another on this "island," but there were some large hollows among the dunes, some of them perfectly bowl-shaped, where the wind seemed confused about its direction and the turmoil of the surf was more distant.

It was in one of these craters that I found the house.

It is a little gray box standing on stilts driven into the sand. Its roof and side walls are shingled and are of almost the same color and texture. The trim around the door is white, as are the shutters, now closed. There is a small porch, two chimneys—one brick and one tin pipe—and a small copper weather vane mounted at one end of the roof ridge. This squeaked dryly in the wind, a faint, piping sound like a lost bird.

I was almost sorry to see the bronze plaque on the house announcing that the Secretary of the Interior had been there a few years ago and had designated the place a "national literary landmark." But something about the cottage seems indifferent to the plaque—indeed, perhaps indifferent to Henry Beston, too. People come and go on this Narrow Land, some leaving a mark where they have passed, some leaving no trace at all. The Cape itself is involved in a greater struggle than the survival of a single house. Each hammer blow of the winter surf counts the time that is left like the knelling of a great geologic clock.

I walked around the house, less interested in its boards and shingles than in the fact that I was there, many summers too late perhaps, but still collecting bits of Cape Cod. The collection was emotionally important once, now it was simply something to tuck away.

I climbed the dune behind the house, heading into the wind, heading for the beach to see the battlefield. I turned once to look at the house, tucked it away in my mind, then lowered my head and bucked my body through a gap in the sand where the wind flowed in a steady torrent, like water through the gates of a dam. On the other side, the sea was in command of everything.

With the inner road along the marsh wholly flooded by now, I decided to walk back to the car by way of the outer beach if I could. The wind was quartering from my right, and it was a force that did not come in puffs and gales like a summer storm but pressed against me unendingly, shoving me along, making my body go faster than my feet.

The sea, when I could turn my face to watch it, was a giant cauldron of suds, hissing and sweeping a concrete-hard beach, its waves crouching and leaping at the shore in a relentless attack. I allowed myself to be propelled along, keeping my eyes down to see what the ocean might have carried ashore—teakwood planks, automobile tires fully inflated on their wheels, large plastic bottles still sealed tight, long bits of synthetic rope in various colors, frayed like the mane of a sea serpent, clothing, a glove, a shoe, a hardhat; and rolling over all was the brown suds of the sea foam, like the head blown off a stein of root beer, skipping and racing ahead of the wind.

Beston had seen it all, I thought. He'd probably walked here, heard the same sounds and understood them.

I could see my car ahead. On higher ground, lights were coming on in the old Coast Guard Station. I had been walking almost two hours. In the summer, I thought, we might have done it in less, but we wouldn't have met the wild things that rule in February.

CRAFTSMAN IN CLAY

I REMEMBER the day Becky picked out her "solid silver ring" at the jewelry store on Commercial Street in Provincetown. She was about nine, I think, and she had a hat which said "Life is Just a Bowl of Cherries" around the brim. Her face was summer toasted, and her big, brown eyes sparkled with pleasure when she looked at all the handmade things in the glass cases—earrings, pins, rings.

"I like that one, Dad," she said, but the young silversmith who was waiting on us said he didn't have one of the plain, wide sterling bands in the right size.

"I'll make one up for you," he said obligingly. "I'll have it ready late this afternoon."

I don't recall what we did, all of us, for the rest of that day, but it probably seemed a long time to Beck before the hour arrived to go back for the ring. When she slipped it on her finger, finally, she was full of pride. Someone had made this pretty thing for her . . . just for her. She twisted the bright, polished circle around and around on her finger. She kept it for years after that. I suppose she may have it still.

Cape Cod was always a place where you could find artsy-craftsy things—leather sandals and belts, well oiled with brass rivets; jewelry; souvenirs made from shells or driftwood or glass fishnet floats; local candy; and, of course, all the oil paintings and watercolors and woodblocks and lithographs and etchings and silkscreen prints that you might be tempted to lug home. Some people called Provincetown an "artists' colony," and some people believed it. I doubt that we ever ran into any bona fide artists during all our summers, unless the sidewalk caricaturists who worked in swift black strokes, or the portraitists who smudged around with pastels qualified. I've been told that there are no good artists left on the Cape and far fewer true craftsmen than the Chamber of Commerce would have you believe.

Harry Holl is a great shaggy man with a graying beard who, some say, is the best potter on Cape Cod, if not the best between Boston and the Bronx. It was a winter day when I stopped by to talk with him at his place in Dennis.

"I came from the Bronx," Holl said, sitting astride his bench, his strong hands manipulating the gray clay on the spinning potter's wheel. "Came up here first in 1948 and got married in Provincetown. Then I went out to Oregon for a while, studied under the G.I. bill, finally came back here to stay in 1952. You could buy property here in Dennis for ten dollars an acre then—and less than that in the winter—but I didn't buy. I didn't have any money. In fact, I couldn't even earn a living right away. Not as an artist anyway. I did other things—carpenter's helper, plumber's assistant, worked in a foundry. . . ."

Holl's place is called Scargo Pottery. It is hidden away in the pines, along the shore of Scargo Lake, a deep gem of an ice-age pond left behind by the melting of a glacial tooth. There is a gallery-showroom where summer crowds browse and buy, and a large workshop where the pottery is made. Holl makes stoneware mostly, tough pieces (because they are fired at high temperature) in muted colors; all sorts of graceful shapes: bowls and plates and covered dishes, vases and wine decanters and mugs.

"But I won't make any ashtrays that say Cape Cod on them," Holl says seriously. "I don't try to make what people want. I make what I'm interested in; it seems to go in cycles from year to year. And the summer people seem to buy whatever I make. I use eight to ten tons of wet clay a year. I never mark anything 'Made on Cape Cod.' "

He was shaping pots now, the special steel tool in his hand cutting ribbons of wet clay from the bottom of each piece, the peelings falling silently, like thick cuttings of lead being turned off a lathe. We sat facing a new area of the shop, a sort of greenhouse with a sloping plastic roof and clear plastic walls. Plants of all varieties were prospering in their clay pots, some blooming even now in winter, some with rich and elegant leaves, dark green and shiny.

"The Cape has a reputation for being a center of crafts," Holl said as he worked. He still has a trace of New York in his accent. "But there really aren't many craftsmen here, you know. Retired people come down here to live and they think they ought to be able to take classes in crafts, but there's no place for them to learn. And the kids aren't taught crafts in the schools here.

"There are only four or five good young craftsmen on the Cape. No weavers. Only one cabinet maker. Several jewelers, a couple of enamelists. Quite a few leather workers. But there's a big resurgence of interest in crafts. The newness of manufactured items is wearing off; the idea of having something made by machine isn't as thrilling as it was forty years ago. People are discovering that having to live with mass-produced things can be tiring, boring. They have no personal quality, these machine-age products. They're cold. People sense this without knowing it, without being able to verbalize it. That's why I think there will be need in the future for thousands of craftsmen—potters, weavers, all of them supplementing industrial production and contributing designs to it as they do now in Italy and Scandinavia.

"I think this is one of the keys to maintaining a society that doesn't self-destruct."

Holl's place is open year round. "Get your book written quick," he says. "Pretty soon there isn't going to be any difference down here, winter or summer. In another ten years, the way things are going, I don't know why anyone would come here."

But not yet; there's time yet, isn't there?

"I start getting ready for next summer right after Labor Day," Holl says, indicating racks full of finished work behind him. But more and more people come down on winter weekends now. They're buying all winter. I don't get as much done as I used to. It's harder to build up an inventory. I think I produce more work in the summer now because I respond to the pressure. There's always a bunch of kids sitting on that bench where you are, watching, and people are buying everything I make. Sometimes on a rainy day in summer we get so mobbed I have to close the place because there's nothing left to sell."

The wheel, motor driven, rumbled softly. Along one wall, large plastic containers were labeled with strange terms: iron chromite, nickel carbonate, soda ash, raw ocher, granular rutile . . . fascinating words which translate into beautiful colors in the heat of the kilns.

"Lot of young people living down here in the winters," Holl went on. "Cooperative living. They rent big old houses and they set up their own food co-ops and their own free university and their own coffee shops. A lot of Cape Codders resent them being here. That's because the young people don't have steady jobs and don't seem to be suffering enough.

"But they work. There are jobs in the supermarkets, and there's woodcutting in the winter. Some of the boys go up to Boston and work as longshoreman for two or three days and come back with $100."

Holl selects two apprentices to work with him each summer. He has many more applicants than he can handle. "I pick the two who are most persistent, who pester me the hardest, who seem most serious—and from whom I think I might learn something myself."

Another ten years and it will be over? Did he mean that?

"Oh, they claim there's enough land out here to continue the present rate of development for another fifty years. But I know what that means," says New York-born Harry Holl. "It means another Long Island.

"All these people who keep coming. A lot of their dreams are bound to end in tragedy." Holl shakes his head, keeps shaking it. "What they don't realize, a lot of them, is that it's a lot easier for a country bumpkin to go to New York City and survive than it is for a city person to come to a place like Cape Cod. Sure, the country boy will get taken in the big city once or twice, but the city folks just don't have the experience or the know-how to take care of themselves out here. They don't know which kind of wood is best for a fireplace, they don't know how to make things or fix things. They can't grow anything. Most of them don't know a seed from a peanut. I know, I went through the whole thing. There's a big difference between coming here for a vacation and coming here to live. Living means all the time. Every month."

Harry Holl's skilled hands were gray from the clay, worn, moist, delicate in their movements, deft. They picked up the soft clay pieces as they would a bird with a broken wing, surely, lovingly. They were hands which had built a man's life. Which could make something beautiful and useful. Which could survive on Cape Cod, no matter how many people come in summer or stay away in winter.

.

PROVINCETOWN'S INN

THE Provincetown Inn is a big, rambling hotel-motel with many rooms, convention facilities, a bowling alley, a big dining room, and murals everywhere, depicting the Provincetown of a century ago. The Inn presides, for that is the word, at the Cape's tip end, just where the Mayflower people are said to have come ashore in 1620. For almost half a century, the Inn has been, physically at least, the biggest thing in town.

We used to go there once a summer for a lobster dinner —the girls in dresses, Chuck all cleaned up—and we would sit in the dining room and look out the big windows as dusk settled over Cape Cod Bay and the harbor lights came on. Sometimes we talked about making a trip back to the Inn "for Thanksgiving dinner," but that's all it ever was, summer talk. We didn't even know whether the place was open in November or not. As I found out later, in the 1950s, it wasn't. In those days, if you had this crazy idea to have Thanksgiving dinner in the place where the Pilgrims first landed, you'd have to bring your own food. Provincetown was as deserted as a boardwalk in a blizzard.

The man who gets a lot of credit for changing all that is Chester Peck, the middle-aged, sometimes grumpy owner-manager of the Provincetown Inn.

"When Chester decided to stay open all year round," a restaurant owner will tell you, "he changed the whole winter scene on the Lower Cape. As soon as people knew there was a comfortable place to stay, no matter what the weather, they started coming out here anytime from Thanksgiving to Easter."

"Riding on my coattails, that's what they're doing, all of these other places," says Mr. Peck.

Like the rest of Cape Cod, the Inn used to be open from Memorial Day to Labor Day, no more, no less. "And you didn't do any business in June at that," Mr. Peck snaps. But since 1967, his Inn has been open twelve months a year and it is usually packed, even on winter weekends.

"We've got 104 rooms and we need 150 more," says Peck. "Until we get 'em, all these other people are living on our overflow."

There is probably some truth to Chester Peck's testy claim. Other, smaller motels stay open year round now and a few of the old white clapboard rooming houses, which are packed in summer, hang out no-vacancy signs on winter weekends. A couple of gift shops and variety stores have also found enough customers to stay open, and five or six restaurants are serving meals.

"Not so long ago," Mr. Peck remembers, "my place was the only place in town you could get breakfast after Labor Day. Thanksgiving? We can't handle it. Booked solid, every year. Why, we've got people coming here instead of going to Florida. They can swim in our heated pool, they can bowl, they can eat plenty of lobster, and they can relax. What more does anybody want?"

Chester Peck may not be solely responsible for the growth of Provincetown's off-season, but the trend has certainly been good to him. He bought the Provincetown Inn as a bank foreclosure in 1935. "I was twenty years old," he says, leaning back in his swivel chair in a cubbyhole office near the kitchen. "I wanted to go into business. I heard I could buy the place for $35,000. All I had was $2500 of my own money, so I borrowed the rest and went to work."

The Inn had twenty-eight rooms in those days and a small dining room.

"We charged eight dollars a night," says Peck. "It was the Depression, and guests were always making wisecracks about just wanting a room, not wanting to buy the place. I had two and a half acres of land here then—got over a hundred today. Course it's a corporation now, but the corporation's me. I own it all."

What about the future of the Cape? How big can the present boom get?

"Bigger yet," says Chester Peck. "Next ten years is going

to be tremendous. We've got to get that four-lane highway extended from Orleans right down here. Eastham's raising hell about it coming through, but we can't do without it.

"There won't be an off-season any more. That's over now. No more off-season rates, either. We'll go to full rates year round. Have to. And I'm going to expand. Going to fill in between here and the breakwater and build more units. Have to. The crowds are going to be tremendous."

Is it the National Park that's doing it?

"Not doing me any good. Or the town either. Bunch of campers come to the Park. They even bring their own food."

After thirty-seven years, does Chester Peck feel like beginning to take it easy, get away from winter, get away from the Inn where he makes his home, travel a little with his wife?

"Haven't been away in four years," he says. "Can't. Too busy here. Where would I want to go anyway? I can't think of anyplace. I've been all over. Far away as the Mississippi. I think I'll stay right here now. You can put on a bathing suit right in your room and walk over and have a swim in our pool anytime. Winter or summer. It's better than the beach."

BELOW
THE LIGHTHOUSE

CAPE COD, like any commercial product, has its trademarks
—cliché symbols printed on paper placemats: lobsters, windmills, gulls. Or colorful lobsterpot markers, fishnets, double-
ended dories, and the codfish itself, which can be found
reproduced on some weathervanes. Perhaps the most universal symbol, however, for the artists and gift-shop operators
and sign painters, is the lighthouse, that classic shape, the
ancient mariners' beacon, standing strong on a point of land.

A lighthouse has a certain mystery about it, I think. Perhaps this is because a *man* lives inside, climbs the iron stairs
to the blinding eye of the light itself, keeps faithful to his
post in all kinds of weather, a sentinel of security in a
dangerous world, the seaman's friend, a special kind of man
who willingly endures loneliness—but why? And how?

One of our summer beaches was called Nauset Light

because a lighthouse stood high on its bluffs. It is a beautifully proportioned light, like a single Greek column, its capital a gleaming 360 degrees of shining glass, its body gracefully tapered. Standing just apart from the tower itself is a plain but sturdy house.

"Is that where he lives, Dad?" one of the kids would always ask. "Is he married? Do his kids live there? Does anyone live in the light itself? It has windows. Can we go in? Would he let us go to the top?"

I didn't know much about lighthouses except that the Coast Guard operated them, I thought. As for visiting the lighthouse keeper, I was sure that was an idea he wouldn't encourage, whoever he was, with several hundred kids on the beach below all ready to invade the light at the first sign of hospitality.

There are four important lighthouses on the Lower Cape —the one at Race Point; a big one, called Cape Cod Light, in Truro; our Nauset Light at Eastham, and Chatham Light at the Cape's elbow. At one time or another, we saw them all, of course, and took their pictures and visited under them at night when the great beacons would rotate relentlessly, flashing their fiery eyes at the sea. But we never went inside, never met a lighthouse keeper, and never touched the mystery of what sort of man he might be.

Something about the off-season on the Cape changes human relationships, draws the few people there closer to one another, as if they had become kin by their mutual

presence on this wintry peninsula. There was no other reason for the man at Nauset Light to open his door and
welcome me. None except that it was a harsh day, and a cold
wind from the sea was climbing the face of the dune and
tearing at the fringe of bayberry bushes and bearberry that
were the eyebrow of the bluff.

"Come in," he said as I thanked him for answering my
knock. He was in his fifties, a tall man, dressed comfortably
in a sweater.

"I've known this light for years," I explained, "but only
in the summer. In all those years, I never met a lighthouse
keeper."

He laughed a big friendly laugh and waved me across the
threshold. "You still haven't met one," he said and laughed
again.

"Aren't you the lighthouse keeper?" I asked, reluctant
now to advance any further.

"Oh, it's all right," he said, "come in anyway. You're not
the first one to make that mistake. In the summer time it
happens almost daily."

His name was Lou Rowell, Colonel L. A. Rowell, USAF,
retired. He bought the house fifteen years ago; the light,
looming about thirty feet from Col. Rowell's front door, is
now fully automated.

"They come up from Chatham about once a month and
service it," Col. Rowell said. "I have nothing to do with it.
In fact, I sometimes forget it's there. The light is so high
that it doesn't shine on us at all."

The house was comfortably furnished with antiques, the bookcases were well stocked, and a neatly groomed poodle shared space with me on the couch.

"Of course, you're right about one thing—this *is* the light keeper's house," Col. Rowell explained. "It was built about 1874, and they obviously understood that it should be mighty strong to stand the weather up here on top of the bluffs. They poured mortar between all the walls and uprights, so the place is pretty snug in the worst blow—but it sure costs twice as much as it should every time I hire a carpenter to fix something."

We looked at old plot plans of the property and at photos of three small lighthouses, the "three sisters of Nauset," which preceded the present light.

"The winters here seem long," Col. Rowell said, "but when summer comes, our real problems begin. People climb up the bluffs from the beach and come to the door and demand to use the telephone—or the toilet.

"I tell them this is a private house, but they won't take my word for that. 'We're taxpayers,' they say, 'and a lighthouse is a public installation and we'd like to use the bathroom.' It's not easy getting rid of them."

I thought of the times the kids had climbed that bluff. "Look up here, Dad. At the top. Now watch us come down." And down they would come, arms flailing, feet kicking up dirt and sand, the plunging sensation squeezing laughter from them.

"The children are the worst," Col. Rowell was saying.

"They tear away some of the bluff every time they do that. Don't they realize that this is something that can never be replaced?"

I said perhaps we didn't.

The next time I went to see a lighthouse keeper, I telephoned first. Cape Cod Light is listed in the directory, and the man who answers is Robert Holbert, Bos'n's Mate 1/C, married, father of five, a twenty-year veteran in the Coast Guard. Along with two other men, he tends one of the most powerful combinations of navigation aids on the east coast of the U.S.; not the least of these is the light itself.

It was midwinter—a moonless, storming night with a forty-mile wind blowing and gusts to sixty. Rain flew horizontally into my headlights as I drove along Route 6 in Truro, and I could feel the tug of the storm through the car's steering. It seemed an appropriate time to visit a lighthouse. If there were ships offshore this night, I thought, they surely needed all the help they could get.

Holbert had said, "Sure enough, come see us," when I called. Then he added, I suppose in fun, "You won't have any trouble finding the place, will you?"

Hardly. I had seen the powerful blink of the light in the night sky for years, had watched its twin beacon sweeping the darkness until I knew just where to look for it. Sometimes I imagined that it made a sound up there in the clouds, like the passage of a giant bullwhip spinning high overhead.

At Truro, I left the main road and headed for the coast. The light grew stronger as I came in under it. It illuminated the rain and made the storm seem worse—as a flash of summer lightning may reveal a fearsome gathering of thunderheads.

Holbert was waiting for the lights of my car. I could see his sturdy figure fighting the wind as he came from the lighted doorway of his house and signaled me to follow him into another building near the base of the tower. We were both a little out of breath as we stomped into a sort of office and unbuttoned our storm coats.

"Hope I'm not interrupting anything important," I said, thinking that a lighthouse keeper must be just a little more anxious on a night like this.

"No problem," he said, sitting down behind his desk.

The sound of the fog horns seemed clearer now that I was inside. It was a deep wail—"A two-second blast every fifteen seconds," Holbert explained. "We run them anytime visibility is less than five miles. You can hear that horn twelve miles at sea—and we've had reports up to twenty-four miles."

The giant air horns are near the edge of the bluff, facing the ocean, but the wind carried their cry inland.

"Doesn't it bother you? Every fifteen seconds like that, all day, all night?" I could feel myself going buggy at the thought.

"Don't even hear them," Holbert said. "Neither does my wife. Have to stop and listen sometimes just to be sure they're runnin' okay."

Holbert and his family have been on the Cape three and a half years. Before that, he was stationed at a lighthouse at the entrance to Galveston Harbor. "Galveston Jetty Light," he said, shaking his head. "Terrible place. Now you take this Cape Cod, though, this here is real good duty."

"Even on a night like this?"

"This is nothing. Had a hundred-mile-an-hour wind here last year. Even that didn't shake anything. The old light, she's solid. Walls three feet thick, all brick."

Holbert sat behind his desk, looking bulky in a short blue jacket. He wore a golf cap.

"I get some golf in almost every day all winter. There's a nine-hole course right by our road here. It's busy all summer, of course, but it's mine all winter. I love the game. I've played in some Armed Forces tournaments, and next year I'm entering the Vermont Open."

The fog horns kept up their warning cry, but now that we were directly under it, the light could not be seen.

"Used to be the most powerful light on the east coast," Holbert explained. "Million candlepower. It was seen as far as forty-four miles. But then they cut the power down to 620,000 candlepower. Ships don't need it that far out any more. Same with our radio beacon. It used to reach to England, but we're down to 150 miles now."

With a certain pride, I thought, he gave me the facts about the 1000-watt bulbs in each of the rotating beacons, how he cleans the big thirty-six-inch lenses and mirrors with straight alcohol once a week. "The glass windows on the tower are the worst problem, though. They frost over in the winter unless I wash 'em regular on the inside. I use straight Prestone. Nothing like it."

Cape Cod Light stands on the highest bluff on the Narrow Land. It is 150 feet from its edge to the beach below, a steep, leg-tearing climb even in summer, a dangerous, eroding place in winter.

"I lost twenty-three feet of bluff in one month last winter. So far this year, it's fifteen feet more. The sea is comin' in all right. Comin' in to get the light. They say she's good for another fifty years here, but I'm not so sure. This sand moves out awful fast when the winter surf eats into it."

The first light, built here in 1798, is gone without a trace. "Out there somewhere," Bos'n' Holbert says, pointing seaward with a grin.

We talked a while, then went back out into the rain. I said thank you, but the wind carried the words away. He just nodded and said something back that I couldn't hear. The horn cried and cried, and the beams from the light thrashed around overhead. I'd seen them from afar on warm nights when they were part of the Cape's summer magic. Now I'd seen them during business hours.

DULCE DOMUM

Our cottage was called Dulce Domum. Sweet Home. I say *our* cottage, although it wasn't really ours. We rented it every year from people who were our neighbors in Connecticut. Twelve summers, if my count is right. So it *became* ours. Every board and squeak of it.

Dulce Domum sits in the pines on a back road in Eastham. It is a small white clapboard house with green trim, and its roofs seem to pitch in several directions. A porch with many windows faces one way. The front door and breezeway face another. A bedroom was added on at one end years ago, and a bathroom usurped part of the breezeway later on. Two generations of outhouses had been out back, the older one eventually taken down, the newer one kept as a tool shed. There is a small pumphouse, doghouse size, in the front yard. And a picnic table, which always wore a red and white checked oilcloth, tacked down at the ends so the breeze wouldn't carry it away.

The place became a part of our lives—a name spoken as affectionately in winter as in summer, a synonym for peace, love, escape, a place that would always be there, innocent and true, a place to go back to . . . for how long? Seemingly forever, I thought. Dulce Domum was timeless, and when we went there, we were never any older than the summer before.

Each year, in August, when we returned, the car doors would burst open and children would race toward the house, hands reaching into the place over the door where the keys were traditionally hidden. Two things always had to be ascertained immediately: what had changed since last year and, of course, what was lovingly the same. A new linoleum floor which the owners installed one year was clearly an improvement, but the kids didn't like it. When cinder blocks replaced cedar poles as supports for the porch they complained that the floor didn't bounce any more when jumped on. And when the kitchen was all gussied up with a new sink and yellow countertops, a little more of Dulce's rustic charm seemed to slip away. But these were small matters. They didn't really interfere with the spell that the cottage cast on all of us. It was a gingerbread house in an enchanted grove, old scrubby pines sheltering it, filtering dappled sunlight onto a thick carpet of cinnamon-colored needles. Sometimes, in the night, a pine cone would fall with a rattle onto the roof and then roll off the edge; when morning came, squirrels would scramble up there, small feet scratching the shingles. If the wind was right, you could smell the smoke from the town dump not far away—nothing objectionable, really, mostly corn husks and paper plates and lobster shells burning. You could also hear the cries of the squadrons of gulls which policed that facility.

The beaches were not far away; about a mile and a half to the bay and the same distance in the other direction to the ocean—a fact which seemed to us to set Dulce apart from all those miles of cottages so neatly drawn up along the shore, with nothing to watch but the sea. Dulce was for more than changing your bathing suit. Dulce was, indeed, Sweet Home.

When all the summers were over, when the first August came that we did not go back, Dulce was one of the things that could not be divided or bequeathed or disbursed or assigned custody to. If it missed the particular tread of our feet or the sound of our voices that year, it would never be explained. We were gone without so much as a goodbye.

When I went back for the first time after that, it was winter. Many times I had driven past Dulce's road, going and coming through Eastham, and I was often tempted to turn off, over the bump where the railroad tracks had been, down to the fork, bearing right, then up the rise to the place where you can first see the outline of the porch through the trees. But always, until this day, I had kept straight on, putting off the encounter as if there would be some embarrassment about it.

Where have you been?

Oh, busy. You know.

Missed you.

Me too.

There had been some snow, but it was almost gone except in the shady spots. I saw lumps of it by the pumphouse as I turned in the driveway. I counted the rhythm of the familiar bumps under the wheels where roots ran on the surface. I stopped the car in the usual place, the door just missing the tree by the usual distance as I opened it to get out.

The plank that reached between two pines to support the kids' swing had come loose at one end, I saw. Sap had run from the holes where the spikes had been. Should be fixed, I thought. And the locust tree still leaned at an odd angle, with the nail in it where we used to hang the dartboard.

I went to the door and reached for the keys, but of course they were not there. "It's January, you old fool," I thought. "Why would the keys be there in January? Anyway, you didn't tell anyone you were coming."

Since I couldn't enter, I started a circuit of the house, looking in the windows, trying to see everything, wanting suddenly to remember.

Chuck's room first, the one at the end. It had been Patrick's room, too, the first year we squeezed his crib in there. The interior of Dulce is unfinished pine with lots of shelves nailed here and there between the studs. I could see the one where Mrs. Baker kept her jigsaw puzzles and another shelf, higher up, where the electric heaters were stored. The white sailboats still sailed on the blue window curtains, and the wall lamp still hung over Chuck's bed where I used to read the goodnight story.

I moved around to the back of the house. More old galvanized nails in the tree where I had stretched a big tarpaulin around our outdoor shower—a five-gallon can, painted red, fitted with a sprinkler head at the bottom, filled with warm water, and hoisted up with a pulley. Even after the owners installed a proper shower in Dulce's bathroom, we remembered, even preferred, the refreshing chill of bathing under a canopy of pines and blue sky.

Another window. The main room. Countless old copies of *Reader's Digest* and Ellery Queen mystery stories where they had always been on shelves. The oil lamp in case of power failure. The iron woodstove. The folding chairs that made a gritty noise when pushed along the sandy floor. The three hooks high in the ridgepole where we used to hang the kites—Spacebird, bat kite, and the old box. The green bottle, filled with sand, that was a doorstop. The tin box with a hinged top, always full of pins and needles and thread.

I crunched snow underfoot when I came around to the porch. The ladder and a small dinghy were still stored in the space underneath. The glass and cork floats still hung in the windows. Mattresses were turned up on edge on the beds—Jenny's on this side, Becky's over there. The blue table would be between them, and four blue chairs and a napkin holder, the shape of an apple, cut from plywood, painted red. When it rained, we had breakfast on this porch.

The rambler-rose vines caught on my sleeve in front of the kitchen window. Their blossoms were pink, I remembered. Two shallow craters in the ground, partially covered now with pine needles, showed where the horseshoe pits had been. The picnic table was turned on its side, the red and white tablecloth still attached. Chains that suspended canvas hammocks between the trees in summer now hung straight down, quivering slightly as the wind shivered the treetops.

A pickup truck rushed by on the road, making a noise that brought me back to January. I saw the driver look at me. Wouldn't the man wonder what I was doing there?

"If someone asks me," I thought, "I'll say I'm checking the property for the owners. And I am, in fact. Looking after an old friend. When I get back, I'll call Harriot Voorhis and tell her all's well with Dulce."

Curiously, in all the years, I'd never asked Gerry and Harriot Voorhis any questions about their summer place. Who had built it? How old was it? Why was it called Dulce Domum? I got the answers to those questions years later, but what we didn't know in those warm young days didn't seem to matter.

Now I looked at the house for the first time as someone else's, a black and white photograph, much sharper in focus than my misty impressionist painting of the past.

Maybe it was better that way.

EPILOGUE

Winter was over now, and because the springtide of people returns to Cape Cod earlier each year, by May I thought no more of returning. Wouldn't it soon be warm again? Wouldn't the whine of automobile tires on hot asphalt soon pierce the Narrow Land, bringing with it another season, another crowd, another gorging, another generation, another army of discoverers, looking and exclaiming, renting and buying, working and playing—and, indeed, probably loving the place to death all over again?

What could I say to them now? Welcome to Cape Cod, all ye who haven't been here before? Let me tell you about my place and my time. Let me show you where I lived and loved. Let me tell you how it was then, before you came here. There was no motel where you are staying, you know. The road was narrower here. Those cedars were smaller, too. An old couple lived in that house that is now a restaurant.

And the restaurant my kids liked is now a place that sells surfboards.

Your children will play on the same beaches that mine did, dig in the same sand, get brown under the same sun. It is your turn. I had mine. My little boy with the butch haircut and the beach shovel is full-grown now and his hair is long. My little girl who chased chipmunks in her nightie before breakfast is tall and ladylike. The dogs we brought with us are both dead. The black cat lives on, probably happy that, at his age, he is no longer transplanted each year to that alien place.

Forgive me if I sound querulous; I am not. The Cape is yours, whoever you are, and I hope you love it as much as I did. I could not go back with you even if you would have me, however, for it is now another season and another play.

Saying goodbye is hard. Like a parting with an old friend, I have lingered over the final handshake. I said, This can't be; I don't yet know you well enough. There is so much more we might say, so much more I'd like to ask. Just the other day one of the kids said, "I wonder what it's like in the winter, Dad?" It *was* just the other day, I'm sure. Why don't I just get the answer to that last question, I said, before I go.

So that's why I came in winter, I suppose. It put off the time when I would leave. It finished my Cape Cod painting. The one there would always be time to finish. It put snow on the shingled cottage roofs. And ice on the beaches. And pale, cold sun on the marsh grass. It is a picture I shall always cherish in the galleries of my mind.

Now my winter is over and your summer begins. It is time for you to commence your own discoveries and time for my quest to end.

Goodbye, Cape Cod.

I love you.